LABOUR AND OTHER QUESTIONS IN SOUTH AFRICA

Labour and Other + +
Questions in South Africa

BEING MAINLY CONSIDERATIONS ON THE RATIONAL AND PROFITABLE TREATMENT OF THE COLOURED RACES LIVING THERE + + +

BY "INDICUS"

NEGRO UNIVERSITIES PRESS
NEW YORK

Originally published in 1903
by T. Fisher Unwin, London

Reprinted 1969 by
Negro Universities Press
A Division of Greenwood Publishing Corp.
New York

SBN 8371-1298-2

PRINTED IN UNITED STATES OF AMERICA

INTRODUCTION

THE tour in South Africa, of which some account is given in the following notes, was undertaken for purely commercial reasons by a gentleman who has large business interests in India. The author, having lived in India for many years, is naturally interested in the welfare of the people of that country, for whom he has much sympathy. He was greatly astonished at the extent to which the Indians have contributed to the prosperity and well-being of South Africa. Nothing that he had seen or heard had given him any idea that such was the case, and many, if not most, Englishmen are no doubt as ill-informed as he was on the subject. He was not less surprised to notice the treatment meted out to Indians and other coloured races in the South African colonies—a treatment which, in his opinion, is as impolitic as it is unjust. This aspect of South African policy being very little noticed in the home press, and its bearing on the future of the colonies being consequently insufficiently appreciated, it occurred to the author that the publication of his notes might be useful in bringing to light the disabilities under which coloured races generally—the educated Hindu in common with the Kaffir—suffer in the South African dominions of His Majesty. The importance of the question has lately, moreover, been greatly increased by the proposal to introduce Asiatic labour on a large scale into the Transvaal. These considerations are the author's excuse for publishing this book.

The conclusions arrived at by the author are not in accord with the views constantly enunciated by a large portion of the London press. These latter are based too much on information that is often wanting in accuracy, and in some cases the writer believes designedly misleading. The pages following will be mainly a record of facts observed by the author, and of conversations with persons of diverse races and various political views ; the sources of information being indicated if not obvious from the context. The opinions given necessarily differ according to the quarter from which they emanated and the experience of the persons who gave them. The inferences deduced will also be found to vary somewhat from time to time as the writer saw new places and made new friends. But though in commenting on facts and conversations some variations in the views expressed occur, the conclusions are in the main the same, and are summarised at the end of the book. The author lost no opportunity of obtaining and recording the opinions of any one who appeared to have real opportunities of gauging the feelings of the inhabitants, white or black, or who had such experience of the country as enabled him to speak with any semblance of authority on past events, or to indicate the best policy for the future.

It is perhaps necessary to say that sympathy for the speaker or appreciation of his personal qualities, however strongly expressed, must not be taken to denote agreement with the opinions enunciated, and that such agreement where stated was, as before mentioned, liable to qualification as further experience was gained. The writer, it may be observed, has no financial interests of any kind in South Africa. The tour extended from early in December, 1902, to the end of March, 1903, and the record commences on board ship between Bombay and Aden.

CONTENTS

CHAPTER I

PAGE

Conversations during the voyage from Bombay to Aden—Remarks as to extension of territory at Aden—Embarkation on a German steamer—Views of passengers on the situation in South Africa—Zanzibar—Influx of coloured men as passengers and crowded state of ship—A railway engineer on Uganda and the German colonists settled there—Character of Mr. Kruger—Mozambique 1

CHAPTER II

Detention at Mozambique owing to an accident to the ship on leaving harbour—Transfer of passengers to a smaller steamer—Conversations with Boer, Dutch, and other passengers—Chinde—Beira—Delagoa Bay—Prosperity of the German line of steamers 15

CHAPTER III

Landing at Durban—Race and labour questions—Natal colonists—Kaffirs—Lack of manufactures—Agriculture and horticulture in a very backward state—Wealth of the colony of Natal mostly due to wars—Benefit derived by Durban from the Transvaal gold discoveries—Skilled labour mostly white, but manual labour almost entirely done by blacks—Difficulty in obtaining a passport for Indian servant to proceed to the Transvaal—Food supply of the colony mostly mported 29

CONTENTS

CHAPTER IV

PAGE

Roman Catholic cathedral—Protector of Immigrants—Durban peculiarities—Scarcity of labour—Objection of whites to do hard manual labour—Native question constantly alluded to, but never defined—Conversation with Indians—Berea—Colonial criticisms of Rhodes and Kitchener—Divine service—Demeanour of military officers—Numbers of whites, Indians and Kaffirs—Tramways in Durban—New Zealanders and Australians—Commercial standing of Indians—All progress in horticulture due to Indians—An American's opinion of the colonists 45

CHAPTER V

Maritzburg—Military not popular with the civil population—Indian landholders—Buildings and roads—Town prosperous owing to the war—Sugar-planter's opinion of Indian coolies—Temperature and climate—Coloured labour indispensable—Mr. Chamberlain—Dutchman's views as to coming events—Police officer's account of the country 65

CHAPTER VI

Ladysmith—Waggon Hill and Cæsar's Camp — Town prosperous—Railway journey to Johannesburg—Building contractor's account of the labour difficulty and rate of wages—Heidelberg railway station—Arrival at Johannesberg 76

CHAPTER VII

Johannesburg—Feeling of despondency and insecurity—Transport difficulty—Sir W. Butler and Lord Milner—Indians in the Transvaal—Climate—White and black labour—Looting during the war — Mr. Chamberlain and the labour question—Kaffir wives—Price of land in Johannesburg—A clergyman's opinion as to the state of the town, also on the manner in which the war was brought about—Increase of prices since the war—Including the Boers, the majority of the white population of Johannesburg came from South-Eastern Europe—The English birds of passage—The coming Kaffir war 81

CHAPTER VIII

PAGE

Journey from Johannesburg to Pretoria—Arrival at Pretoria—Kruger's house and church—Bad effects of the war—Pretoria clean, well laid out, and apparently prosperous—Indian shopkeepers especially useful to the Boers — Some of the Indians prosperous, others barely make a living—Views of an Englishman who had been twelve years in the country 99

CHAPTER IX

Return to Johannesburg—Permit regulations fail to exclude undesirables, whilst they cause much inconvenience—Journey from Johannesburg to Capetown—A railway manager on black labour—His surprise on learning that, in India, coloured people are not subject to restrictive regulations—Repudiation of Cape Colony public debt under discussion previous to gold discoveries in South Africa—Boers predominate in Pretoria and thence to Capetown prevail 106

CHAPTER X

Capetown—Hotel—Further remarks on incidents during railway journey from Johannesburg to Capetown—Dutch and English inhabitants of Capetown apparently irreconcilable—Cape Colony very prosperous as the result of expenditure incurred on the war—Cheap labour indispensable but lower class whites opposed to immigration—Agriculture very backward—Dutch must, by force of numbers, eventually rule—Indians, Malays, and other coloured races better treated in Capetown than elsewhere in South Africa—Fruit excellent—English Church not flourishing—Simonstown—Dutch the prevailing language in Capetown, and spoken by the coloured races—Sir W. Butler—Wynberg—Cape Civil Service—Constantia—Farming prospects in South Africa—Mr. Chamberlain's visit—Dutchman on the situation in Cape Colony and the Transvaal—Municipal matters . 111

CHAPTER XI

Voyage home—A doctor on the concentration camps—Mr. Chamberlain's speeches to Progressives at Capetown not fully reported—An American on Kaffirs, colonials, and others—A colonial lady's views—The

PAGE

coming native war—Capabilities of Kaffirs—Slackness in business houses at Capetown—The Transvaal Railway Company—Indians indispensable in Natal—Boers more united and confident than they were before the war—Military officer's objection to South Africa—A colonial's view of the situation—Coloured races in Cape Colony—Nurse's experience—Madeira 127

CHAPTER XII

Summary and Author's Conclusions 139

Labour and Other Questions in South Africa

CHAPTER I

Conversations during the voyage from Bombay to Aden—Remarks as to extension of territory at Aden—Embarkation on a German steamer—Views of passengers on the situation in South Africa—Zanzibar—Influx of coloured men as passengers and crowded state of ship—A railway engineer on Uganda and the German colonists settled there—Character of Mr. Kruger—Mozambique.

MY first opportunity for discussing South Africa occurred on the steamer with a young gentleman who may be described as No. I. He was a fine, handsome young barbarian of ultra-British sentiments and tastes, untempered apparently by the remotest conceptions of abstract justice or consideration for others, but of unusual experience for a subaltern, as he had been for some years in Australia, the Southern States of America, India, and South Africa before the war, and had won a commission in a British regiment, in which he was then serving. He was of opinion that England could not get on without its colonies, and that it must be solely guided in its treatment of them, by what they themselves demand. Any attempt, he said, to interfere in South Africa, on the question of according fresh rights or privileges to coloured races, even East Indians, would cause separation. He therefore does not believe that England, whatever it may have said in the past, will attempt anything of the kind, and personally he would far rather lose India than offend the South African colonists. He mentioned that although Mr. Chamberlain had disallowed the Exclusion of Asiatics Bill in Australia, yet he has allowed the Language (Undesirable Colonist) Act (admittedly only a trick to get out of an awkward difficulty) to be brought into force, and that he had no doubt at all that he would do the same in South Africa. There, the colonists desire that all natives of India shall be sent back after five years' indentures, whatever the feeling in India may be on the subject. He thinks that, provided the English Government acts in accordance with colonial views—and he is unable to conceive them not doing so—South Africa will settle down. It is not, he thinks, understood in England, how near a move towards independence came about before the raid, when many colonists were moving in that direction.

My next conversation was with a gentleman, who may be designated as No. II., apparently an Afrikander, who said that he had chiefly lived in South Africa, and had been employed in the largest mines there. He had been travelling for two years or more, mostly in the East. It is not unlikely that he was a Boer prisoner, whose evidence should therefore be received with caution. He says that the war was an improper one, brought about by interested parties, the Boer farmers being ignorant of the facts, whilst the Hollanders, seeing the *rapprochement* that was rapidly forming between the Boers and the English, feared that they might lose their places. He thinks that all will settle down, if Government does not force matters, and lead the Boers to think that they will be worse off under the new *régime* than under the old one. Much caution and avoidance of anything like bullying is necessary. From what he hears, he thinks that it will take ten years for the new colonies to regain the position they had attained before the war. Absolutely the backbone of the country is mining, and the ore being all low grade will not pay for white labour, which costs ten shillings a day at the lowest, whilst Kaffirs, whose mining efficiency, compared with the white man, may be taken as three to five, will on the average work for two shillings a day. At present Kaffirs ask for a higher wage, as they have made money during the war, and until the Boer farmers are re-established, they will find that growing farm produce is more profitable than mining. Formerly each Kaffir Chief or King was compelled to force his subjects to work for three months every year in the mines. This practice, it is supposed, will now be stopped. The work in the mines is trying, and Kaffirs are used up in a very few years. They are, as regards mining work at least, a stupid race, and cannot be taught the simplest fitting work, which is done by white men. Under the Transvaal Government the Boers, besides paying taxes, were commandeered for any native war, and they will appreciate being freed from this liability. If tenderly treated at first they will in time become loyal to the new Government. He knew some farmers who had four thousand head of cattle before the war, whilst now they probably had none.

It may here be mentioned that at Aden, where we stopped for a few days, there is said to be only one business firm which is really English—the remainder are German, American, and Italian. The Germans work for very low salaries, such as no Englishman would accept. The place is rather going backward than forward, as the size of steamers increases. Aden has no very definite boundaries, and the usual process of land-grabbing seems to be just now going on. It is claimed by the British officials that the boundary (or sphere of exclusive influence at least) extends to one hundred and fifty miles inland from the port, and they are clamouring for a railway to the foot of the hills which occur at that distance from Aden, and where, besides the attraction of a comparatively cool climate, potatoes and vegetables can be grown.

After a few days a new start was made in a large German steamer, and I found myself at the saloon table next to a lady who lives at Johannesburg. She had had a wet summer at home and was glad to be returning to the sun. Her description of Johannesburg is not encouraging. Houses with five or six rooms are said to rent at £30 to £40 a month, and many people are living in tents. She laughingly observed that the different white races would now have to get on better together, but a general disinclination, on the part of South Africans, to allude to such matters was observable; at any rate they never, of their own accord, broach the subject. There are seventeen different nationalities on board the ship, chiefly Levantines and Italians, the latter intending to work on the railways. The captain and officers discourage conversation on politics and religion, and consequently during the whole of the war, and since, there has never been unpleasantness on board. The captain thinks that Boers, Britishers, and Uitlanders alike feel it a great relief to come on board and leave political strife behind them. My own observation is to the same effect.

I may introduce No. III. as a burgher who was formerly in the service of the Transvaal Government, but who moved to Cape Colony on account of his health a year or two before the war. He was a gentlemanly man, who before the war was rich, but who has lost a good deal of his property. He stated that the country was "entirely ruined," as I should find out for myself. He reckoned his own losses in five figures, his farm having been turned into a fort without warning, and all his trees felled and burnt. He was, by his own account, treated most cavalierly, and apparently foolishly, for he was not even allowed to fell the trees for sale as firewood for which he could have got £400. He has also lost heavily in Pretoria where he has many houses, two of which were taken, as they stood, for two officers. A widow living in one of the houses was turned out at twenty-four hours' notice, without being allowed to remove her effects, and forthwith two English ladies were installed therein and lived there for months without paying any rent. This happened when Lord Roberts arrived. My friend intends to sell his property, in

Pretoria and elsewhere in the Transvaal, on account of the heavy taxation which he expects will be imposed, but he has no doubt that Pretoria will remain the capital of the Transvaal.

The war was, in his opinion, brought on by the newspapers, and he only blamed the British for permitting themselves to be so completely befooled. He speaks well of some of the British Cape Ministers, who are said to have administered rebukes to Lord Milner, and he seems to expect that the latter will leave the Cape in a few years time with his reputation gone. He further expressed the opinion that Mr. Chamberlain was not blameless in respect to the raid, adding that remarks to this effect had been openly made by the late Mr. Rhodes on his return to the Cape. In alluding to Lord Milner's probable future, he said, "The Dutch are a very peculiar people—very peculiar." In making this remark his tone and manner altered so much that I thought it very significant. He also said that the natives of India were unpopular in South Africa, but admitted that their unpopularity was mainly due to jealousy, since they were industrious, quiet, and docile. But the Indians took away their savings, and the smaller white men could not work for the wages they are glad to get. The bigger colonists do not object to them so much, and Natal would simply be a desert without them. The labour question is a very hard one, and he believes that the most likely solution of the difficulty in working the poor grade ores of the Transvaal at a profit lies in the importation of Chinamen. On his Cape (Western) farm and vineyard he employs half-castes, who are, he finds, a drunken, thieving, and irregular-working lot of men, and almost impossible as servants.

My next informant, No. IV., I may describe as a German doctor, who was for seven years in the Transvaal, but left eighteen months ago when he and his wife lost their nerve. He is now returning with a nice little child. He is very bitter against newspapers in general, and hopes they will in future have less influence. The Berlin newspapers he declares are all owned by Jews. The South

African newspapers did enormous harm, and their news was, he avers, frequently deliberately false. Pretoria is, he thinks, sure to be the capital of the colony, because Johannesburg is simply a corrupt Bourse. The new Government, he does not doubt, will be more corrupt than the old one, where clerks on £300 a year were often bribed with an equal amount.

No. V., a lady, wife of one of the gentlemen mentioned above, says that the bad government of Kruger was a mere pretext for strife. Lord Milner considered that it was a question of a Boer or British South Africa, and so he determined to bring on war. But she is not sure that the matter is more than half over yet. The labour question must be settled, or the mines will close, and the Transvaal will be ruined. The importation of Chinese will, she thinks, settle the difficulty, and the opposition to that measure is based, in her opinion, on sentiment only. Mine-owners are finding that a strong Government is very different to a Boer one, and they already see and fear a stricter *régime*. There were, it is true, liquor laws before the war, but they were largely inoperative. After the war an effort was made to reduce wages, but the Kaffirs cannot now get liquor, so they simply will not come in. The general native question is a most difficult one. It is not that the natives want war; they do not, for the simple reason that the Basutos alone are armed. The natives do not, however, wish to work underground, and they can live quite well without doing so. In Cape Colony the coloured people have votes, and in the other colonies some of them are beginning to be educated, and to desire votes also. In Natal there are more Indians than whites, and the lady thinks that unless the latter will do manual labour themselves (which she thinks they might do) it is foolish and unreasonable to cry out against the Indians.

No. VI., a Dutch doctor, an unhappy-looking man who speaks English, is going to Durban, and thence to London, to try to get an English medical diploma, as only such are now recognised in the Transvaal, where he practised before and during the war. He is naturally somewhat hipped, being no longer a young man. He represents the Boer, though usually most hospitable, as no longer willing to entertain Britishers, and often unable to do so. The feeling, according to him, has arisen, not so much on account of the war itself as the way in which it was carried on. At present the Boers are greatly enraged, and it may take many years to eradicate the bitter animosity that is now prevalent. Before the war, Boers were pleased to be mistaken for Britishers, but that day has passed away. Asked pointedly what he thought of the future, he said that the British were, he considered, too optimistic. Boers are still Boers, and history will repeat itself. He thought that Mr. Chamberlain had made a fatal mistake in beginning the war, and also in the method of warfare adopted. His own opinion was that the late war had ensured the future independence of South Africa. He did not see why the example of the United States of America should not be followed, whilst even Australia appeared to be moving in this direction, having the Southern Cross, so he was told, on its flag.

The same opinion is held by No. III. He says plainly that he does not believe that the two races will ever unite now, and he doubts whether they would have done so, even if there had not been war. The Dutch, he says, will never be the *under dog* if they are in the majority, though quite willing to submit so long as they are in a minority. The English must do the same, but they will never do so, and are encouraged in this spirit by Lord Milner, who is saturated with British prejudice. No. III. devoutly hopes that Mr. Chamberlain may promote Lord Milner to some appointment that will necessitate his leaving South Africa. He says that his friends are now in a deplorable state—families divided, besides material losses; and he thinks, at times, of moving with his family to the United States of America, but his friends are endeavouring to prevent his doing so. An Afrikander, he says, means a man born in the Cape, of Dutch descent. Those of English descent he would call either British or colonials.

No. II. says that he has no fear of not being permitted to proceed to the Transvaal, as he has a permit from London, but he may have difficulty in getting work there if the Board of Mines boycott ex-burghers. Such, he considers, now that they have taken the oath and are British subjects, ought to receive perfectly fair and equal treatment. He is obviously, however, doubtful as to how far this treatment will be given, and hence his low spirits. The Boers, he says, are all ruined. Those who had saved had their wealth either in coin or cattle, and they have lost everything; so that all the elders can look for is bread and cheese till death releases them. He had worked for Rhodes, who had 40,000 men under him, for seventeen years.

The ship touched at Tanga, Dar-es-Salaam, and Zanzibar, regarding which no remarks are necessary, except that they are Indian-looking and have the reputation of being unhealthy. During our stay in port, the gentlemen to whom I have previously referred frequently conversed with me. Their view is that before the war the Germans and other foreigners in the Transvaal were neither pro-Boer nor anti-English, but strongly in favour of Kruger on account of his anti-capitalist policy. The monied English and Americans, who already ruled in Kimberley, formed the opposition in the Transvaal, the French and Germans taking the other side. Kruger would not have allowed a single gold-mine to be opened if he could have prevented it, so the foreign population, not connected with the monied ring, joined him. No. IV. says that the Boers will never take up arms again, but the war has had the effect of joining the Dutch population of the Cape, the Orange Free State, and the Transvaal in a way never before approached, or indeed possible. They will bide their time, get self-government, and then vote for independence. No. IV. is apparently certain on this point, but he may be prejudiced, as such a solution would no doubt suit foreigners best. Practical independence, at least if their views correctly describe the state of affairs, seems to me to be a certainty eventually, and the best solution of the difficulties which beset the grave problem called into existence by the war. It is already enjoyed by other colonies.

The Boers are, he says, very bitter, because even already the peace terms have been broken. The £3,000,000 grant, according to their belief, is passing largely into the hands of Boer blacklegs, whilst the amnesty, which it was separately promised should be granted to Cape rebels, at the Coronation, has not been allowed. No. IV. further says that it is absurd to keep a large army in South Africa. If the Boers are well treated, and the peace terms are loyally carried out, the Dutch will quietly await the results that will follow the inevitable increase in their numbers, which must, eventually, give them most votes. Nothing more can be hoped for. He calculates the probable expenditure on the Transvaal and Orange Colony at three times the expenditure incurred previous to the war—£10,000,000 a year against £3,000,000. He also says that the Transvaal Republic did not arm before the Jameson raid, and that they made no secret of their military preparations after that event. Their armaments were largely supplied by well-known British firms, whom, he avers, continued to supply them after war had been declared; and this, I may add, was several times told me by men with widely differing sympathies, and who obtained their information from altogether different sources. No. IV., it seems, had charge of a hospital during the war, and was very successful with dysentery and enteric patients, but much less so with malarious fever. He was thanked by the British Commander-in-Chief, but remarked that he did not think that he deserved any special thanks for simply doing his duty.

No. III., in speaking of Cape half-castes, said that they, equally with whites, objected to manual labour in South Africa. They come to him, work fairly well for three or four days, and then wish to superintend only, inquiring, "Where are the 'boys'?" They are, he says, always pronounced Jingoes, if of British descent. The same feeling as regards work exists, in quite as strong a degree, in men of Dutch descent, who inherit it from the slave-holding days. Mixed with them are descendants of the original British settlers, some of whom now only speak Taal, and refuse to give evidence in any other tongue. The colonists from Great Britain, as a rule, work better, their almost universal aim being to possess a bit of land, no matter how worthless. The old Dutch element despises hand-work and all trades, their idea being to teach their children to ride, shoot, and farm only. They would probably re-establish slavery if they could, though they repudiate any such desire. The apprentice system, however, shows their tendency in this direction. No. III. stated that he believed the Kaffirs would only do a reasonable amount of work, under what was practically some form of slavery. Kind treatment should be secured, but he was afraid that no system of slavery could, unfortunately, guarantee proper treatment.

No. IV. again referred to the necessity of treating the Boers with greater tact than had hitherto been used, and of avoiding wounding their susceptibilities. He thought the British were not well advised in removing the Boer coats-of-arms from the public buildings, even before the war was over; and he considered that they should have completed, and not stopped the Kruger memorial. He thought that of the higher British officials Lord Kitchener had shown more good feeling than any one else in his dealings with the Boers, and he believed that if he (Lord Kitchener) had been left a free hand, the war would have come to an end much sooner than it did.

At Zanzibar several hundreds of negroes and natives of India came on board the ship bound for Durban and Port Elizabeth. The Indians are a very clean, tidy lot of Suratis, apparently paying their own way with a view to eventually getting to Johannesburg. It seems to be doubtful if they will do so, as there is a strong animus, amongst the Transvaal whites, against such frugal, industrious and enterprising competitors. The upper-class colonists are acting very much to their own disadvantage in not supporting men who would in every way be a source of wealth to the colony. The negroes are dirty and noisy, and are said to be going to work in the mines, or in the port works of Durban, or on the railways. A visit to the town of Zanzibar showed the streets to be very narrow, almost as much so as in Canton, the place being hotter than Bombay, and abounding in fruit. The trade is mostly in the hands of natives of India, Parsees, Goanese, Borahs, and Khojahs. Here, as in all the ports yet called at, there is great evidence of Roman Catholic enterprise and devotion. The ship is simply crammed—the deck passengers have no room to lie down; and there are no proper sanitary arrangements.

One of the passengers, who came on board at Zanzibar, is an engineer on the Uganda Railway. He gives the natives of India working thereon a very bad name, probably owing to their being misunderstood and mismanaged. He explained that British East Africa, which runs from the coast to Lake Victoria Nyanza, is quite a distinct Government from Uganda, which takes in the country beyond the lake. His opinion of the late and present Governor of British East Africa is not high, but he speaks more favourably of the present Administrator of Uganda. The railway has been open to the lake for some time, but in places it is still temporary. It is not expected that it will pay for the next fifteen years at least. He could give no good reason for its construction. In the two territories there may be five hundred Europeans, including Government servants. He was full of the old story about the neglect of Government to assist the new country, and the flocking in of foreigners, especially Germans, to possess what we had won. He, however, admitted that, but for these same Germans, there would be no European non-officials at all, and that it might therefore pay Government to let others do what Britishers no longer seem to have the stomach for. He even went further, and when pressed admitted that contact with Germans in East Africa had caused him very largely to change his mind, and had led him, unwillingly, rather to admire the Teutonic character. He stated that for fifty miles from the lake to within two hundred miles of the coast the climate is good—quite suitable for Europeans; but he, at the same time, admitted that Britishers would not be in the least likely to go and settle there. It was thus easy to deduce, from his own showing, that this newly-grabbed East Africa and Uganda must be either peopled with foreigners or remain unoccupied, save by natives of the country and a few officials. It is not clear what England has gained by her forward policy in these parts. In German East Africa, as in British East Africa, there is no discrimination, the same customs duties being charged to all, irrespective of the country of origin or export of the merchandise.

In a further conversation with No. III. the character and conduct of Mr. Kruger were discussed. The main question, from my point of view, was whether he was the thief his enemies alleged him to be. The reply was that Kruger was not immaculate as a ruler, though his fault was not in helping himself, but in allowing those under him to be corrupt. In a poor country, suddenly enriched, bribery and corruption were certain to be rampant, if not reined in with the tight hand of a very strong Government. Kruger failed to exercise the stern repression required, but so far as he himself was concerned his pay and the profits from his farms quite sufficiently accounted for his fortune. He lived on £500 a year, and he was paid £8,000 as President of the Republic—latterly £7,000 plus £300 allowance.

The Boers, on board, have Dutch newspapers which are not pleasant reading for Englishmen, whether true or otherwise. In one of them there is a detailed account of certain Lancers driving Boer prisoners ahead of them, first pig-sticking them, and then lemon-cutting them, in a very brutal manner. He says that No. II. admits that in one case the Boers fired on an ambulance, but this was because during a two days' armistice to bury the dead the British attached the guns, which they had left behind, to the ambulance waggons in which they had collected their wounded, with the intention of dragging them off. This action brought on the fire, which was, of course, deserved, if the facts were as stated.

No. III. agrees with me, however, that there must be individual cases of blackguardism in all armies, and he admits that there were a few cases of Boers killing their prisoners. Accusations of this kind, from either side, should be received with great caution. The war, he again insists, has united the Dutch throughout South Africa to an extent never before approached. Before the war the Cape, Orange River, and Transvaal Dutch were by no means on friendly terms; in fact, they were frequently at almost open war. He hopes that for the future they will pull together, but so far as he can judge there is no chance of their again quarrelling. He had two brothers who passed through the war uninjured. He has lent me Kruger's Life which, to my mind, although I hear it spoken of as stupid, is not a pleasant study for an Englishman. A German on board, who has lived in the Transvaal, describes the Boers as simple people with excellent mental abilities, if cultivated, as they are now likely to be. He thinks that it would be foolish to stop teaching the Dutch language in Government schools, as private schools would then spring up. The German schools in the Transvaal are already extremely popular. No. III. does not lay much stress on the language question, probably because he speaks English fluently, and uses it equally with Dutch in his own family.

Mozambique appears to me to be just like other Portuguese towns, very clean and tidy, and the people apparently all comfortably off, but with no signs of wealth, trade, or activity. The fort, five hundred years old, is interesting. It is used as a prison, largely for Indians from Goa. Rain water is stored for the use of the inmates, the town people depending for their supply on rain also. The wells are brackish. As at other places on the coast of East Africa, Bombay Indians, (Borahs, Bhattias, and Khojas) abound, and carry on nearly all the trade. One of the latter said that trade was so bad that he meant shortly to go on to Durban, with a view to proceeding as soon as he could to Johannesburg, to which place numbers of these people are making their way. He complained of the license and other taxes which he said the trade of Mozambique could not support. The negroes live in comfortable wattle and thatched huts, and their quarters seemed to be clean. The roads were lighted at night, and were themselves well kept. Rickshaws are the chief means of locomotion.

CHAPTER II

Detention at Mozambique owing to an accident to the ship on leaving harbour—Transfer of passengers to a smaller steamer—Conversations with Boer, Dutch, and other passengers—Chinde—Beira—Delagoa Bay—Prosperity of the German line of steamers.

THE harbour of Mozambique is a difficult one to get out of, and we soon had ample experience on this point, as about midnight the ship, which had left just two hours previously, touched bottom and stopped. She, however, soon righted herself, except for a slight list to the starboard side. There was some commotion, ladies appearing in their nightdresses. One was said to have fainted. Seeing that nothing was to be done, I turned in and slept till morning, when my servant called me. Luckily the weather was calm. On arrival on deck I found that we were on our way back to Mozambique, with some of the water-tight compartments leaking.

Before the vessel struck, a Boer was giving me his views as to Mr. Kruger, whom he represented as quite an uneducated man, but of good principle and truly loyal to his country. He could not understand why the British abused him, and spoke of him as being very humane, in exemplification of which trait he mentioned that he was present when a report arrived that a number of British prisoners had been taken, whom it was proposed to put in a very cramped place, to save sentries. Mr. Kruger at once forbade this, saying that he was not a barbarian. He observed that we must ourselves show mercy, that we may receive God's mercy. My Boer informant said that he had noticed that age was beginning to tell on Mr. Kruger, and that in conversation he often repeated himself. His eyesight had, however, improved. He had seen him lately.

On arrival at Mozambique, it was found that the bow of the vessel was down some five feet, and that two of the water-tight compartments were full of water. We were favoured by fortune in getting back to Mozambique, as the ship was steadily making water, and the boats were not sufficient to take off one-fourth of the persons on board. There were a thousand souls, all told, on board and to add to our discomforts fresh water for baths was no longer forthcoming. The weather was decidedly warm, with no breeze, very trying to people not used to a tropical climate. The coral reef, on which the ship struck, is said to have grown a good deal since the Portuguese charts were completed.

Another Dutch doctor had a long conversation with me. He is apparently a man of considerable private means, who joined the Boers for service in his professional capacity, and was one of four who remained with them throughout the war. He is an enthusiastic Dutchman of thirty years of age, but he looks to be forty-two at least. The privations he underwent during the war may partly account for his looking so much older than he really is. He makes no secret of his bitter antagonism to the English. His opinion is that the Boers will never give up the Dutch language, chiefly because their Bible is in High Dutch, and they are an extremely religious people. He said with a laugh, "I really believe that they think the Almighty understands the Dutch language only." He said that the Boers would learn English as well as Dutch, as it was necessary for business purposes, but that their home language would, to a certainty, remain Dutch.

In discussing the education question with a Boer, who is returning from an unsuccessful expedition to Dar-es-Salaam to purchase donkeys for the Transvaal, he expressed a strong opinion that the Boers should learn French and German. The Bloemfontein College, in which Latin, Greek, Mathematics, and English were only taught, should, he considered, be avoided. Another Boer, however, did not agree, considering that Dutch and English and some scientific knowledge of farming was the best preparation for life in the Transvaal.

On all hands I am told that farming in South Africa is different from farming elsewhere, and that it must be learnt on the spot and when young. The life is solitary and rough. The pests, cattle diseases, droughts, locusts, and so on, to be combated are legion, and require an intimate local knowledge that no new-comer has any idea of. Lord Milner's idea of small farms of two hundred acres each meets with no favour amongst the Boers. One will have a supply of water, the next in some seasons none at all. Even a Boer could not possibly make a living on such a farm. All will certainly fail. The Boer does not pay his Kaffirs in money, of which he has seldom much himself, but he feeds them, and he gives them a certain acreage of each crop for themselves. They appear to be treated considerately, and not unkindly.

Returning to the Dutch doctor, he has an extremely poor opinion of our army, as seen in South Africa. The men, he says, were lamentably wanting in discipline, hardly ever saluting their officers, for whom they seemed to entertain little respect. They had no power of initiative. When the Boers had to storm a position, they knew that when in close quarters the British fire would go right over their heads, as in point of fact it nearly always did. Tommy Atkins never changed his sights without orders to do so, and rifles picked up usually had their sights fixed for long ranges. They could not hear the words of command, and would not alter the sights without. Many of the officers were new to army life, and according to the Dutch, utterly inefficient. Also he thinks that the men would have fought better in a better cause, as they frequently said when taken prisoners, "Well, we are not fighting for our country as you are." One man was to his own knowledge taken prisoner four times, twice on successive days. He also said that the amount of baggage carried was simply ridiculous. Whenever the Boers took a position they thought, from what they found there, that a picnic had just taken place. It would have been a big feast for the Boers. The doctor, whether right or wrong—and though highly prejudiced, he is an able, well-educated, and thoughtful man—evidently believes that, on account of the above evils, our army could not stand against either a French or German army of to-day. As a result of the South African war, this no doubt is the prevailing continental opinion. The doctor was surprised to hear me talk of the Canadian French, whom he believed talked and thought in English. I said that the English newspapers always wrote in that erroneous strain about them, and probably believed it. He laughed and said, "Why they even now believe that the Dutch in South Africa are loyal."

In regard to the accident, it is sufficient to say here that we were detained in Mozambique six days, and then sent on in a smaller steamer which was brought from Beira. The discomforts experienced by all classes of passengers were extreme, and the assistance rendered by the Portuguese authorities nil. A French man-of-war was, on the contrary, very helpful, her divers making repeated examination of the hull. Fortunately for our comfort the negroes were left behind, but as the Indians came on, the ship was terribly overcrowded. Native passengers in these steamers have a very bad time of it—no place to lie down, and no proper facilities for cooking, many of them living on fruit for the whole voyage. They are also kept at intermediate ports, when they have to change ships, for an indefinite time. The ships' officers do not attempt to deny their sufferings, but try to defend themselves by saying that British ships in this trade are no better.

Another foreigner, a Russian subject, though colonial born, who had been in practice at Johannesburg, says that he does not think that South Africa will settle down for many years. The Dutch, he says, take the gloomiest view of their position, and do not appear to be inclined to make the best of the situation. To an inquiry as to why they should do so, he replied that they seem to forget that they were a good deal to blame for it themselves.

A young Boer, who had been with the passenger who tried to buy donkeys for the Transvaal, proved to be an interesting character. His personality was attractive, and he had a fresh ingenuousness of appearance and manner that was very taking. He was pointed out to me as a good example of a good type of a Boer. The boy, it seems, knows a fair amount of English and German, and has read many of the best books in all three languages. He tells me that he is a Boer farmer, but has been at school for many years in Pretoria. On inquiry as to the relative attractiveness of country and town life, he replied with energy that farm life was his choice. He said that he did not think that any one who had ever lived on a farm ever afterwards cared for town life. He hopes soon to join his younger brother on one of his father's twelve farms in the Middleburg district. His father's head farm is known as Leufontain, and seventy-five miles from the nearest railway station. His father works this farm, and his married brother the next best farm, the latter going in for cattle-breeding, whilst he and his brother intend to grow wheat. Their farm is of about 5,000 acres in extent, on the lower or Bush Veldt, where there are scattered bushes with spots of good earth here and there, which can be cultivated with mealies, wheat, potatoes, onions, and so on. The farmer's life is to be up at 5 a.m., when coffee is taken, work till 9 a.m., when breakfast follows. After breakfast work till 1 p.m. (dinner time), then work till 5 p.m., and in bed at 9 p.m. My informant, however, kept up till 11 p.m. in order to read. With this life he was absolutely contented and happy, his tastes lying in the direction of watching crops growing rather than breeding cattle. The other nine of his father's farms are occupied by poor Boers or Beiwohners, who cannot afford to pay rent and build their own houses. All their houses are now burnt, only the walls still standing, but they hope soon, he says, to rebuild. It is different, however, with respect to the orchards and young fruit-trees, brought from Europe some eight years ago, which have been utterly destroyed, and will take time to restore. So also the young plantations have been all cut down without, he says, any excuse, because they could not serve to feed our enemies. This spirit of wanton destructiveness is a change for the worse, and was exemplified in the Tirah campaign, during which grand old trees, which were the pride of Mohammedan mosques, were destroyed. My friend is very anxious to learn what has happened since he left home, when things were much at a standstill, waiting for Mr. Chamberlain's visit. Lord Milner, he says, is hated by the Dutch, whom in one speech he openly said he meant to extinguish, nor does he think his lordship is much liked by the other side. The war, in his opinion, will not have the effect of extinguishing the Boers, as was anticipated; possibly—nay, probably—the contrary, as it had joined the Boers and the colonials, by whom he meant the Dutch colonials, in a way that had never been the case before, although it was natural in people of one family.

Our new ship is cleaner and more comfortable than the old one, chiefly owing to the absence of the negroes, who were very noisy. There are two Parsee carpenters on board who are going to look for work at East London. They have lately returned from a fifteen months' engagement at a sugar factory in Fiji, of which place they speak well. They got £10 a month and lived on £2, European carpenters getting £15 to £20.

We touched at Chinde, the port for the Congo, British East Africa, parts of Rhodesia, and German East Africa. It has more trade than Mozambique or Dar-es-Salaam. We were met, about ten miles outside Chinde, by a small vessel which only draws nine feet of water. It is a very difficult port to get into, as there is a long bar with shallow water up to ten miles out, and it is also affected by the Zambesi river, which runs out here. The Belgian Congo expedition left us here, with a large amount of baggage, packed in boxes, for land transport. They are commanded by a retired major of the Belgian army, and are nearly all engineers. Their object is to survey a railway from the Congo State to the West Coast of Africa. After the baggage had been hoisted over, the passengers were slung over in baskets, as has often to be done at Durban and other places on this coast. Just before we reached Chinde there was a funeral on board, that of a little girl five years old. Her illness was probably brought on by eating stale fruit, and night chills, being unused to the profuse perspiration induced by the tropical heat.

No. IV. spoke to me about his permit, regarding which he is anxious. He says that under the Kruger Government his whole annual taxation, exclusive of the 11 per cent. import duty, was 18s. 6d. a year, whilst the new Government takes £5 18s. 6d., which sum, he admits, is not excessive. He, however, insists that the outcry of excessive taxation under the Boer Government was absurd, the rich mining population getting off easiest. The result of the increased taxation is, he hears, that a large proportion of the mining population of Johannesburg are joining the Dutch party, the influence of which has been greatly increased by the war. Unlike the majority of foreigners with whom I have talked, No. IV. is quite unbiassed, and tried, during the war, to maintain a perfectly neutral position, which Mr. Chamberlain's despatches, he states, made very difficult at times. He says that the Boers are, as a rule, quite uneducated, and can talk of nothing except the pedigree of a bull or some similar topic, which they will discuss for hours. Their want of education makes living amongst them very trying. But he says they are usually to be trusted. My young friend, he says, may be taken as a fair representative of one kind of them, whilst another man he pointed out was, he said, a sample of a Boer he does *not* like, and would not trust.

The Boer whom No. IV. did not like had a conversation with me in the evening. He said that he did not expect Mr. Chamberlain's visit would have much effect. Mr. Chamberlain would probably do little but make speeches, and try to smooth down the Boers, whose chief concern is as to the taxes they will be called on to pay. Until this point is settled, talking will do little good. The best solution of the South African problem would be to hold the ports and let South Africa govern itself. Such a step could not be expected at once, because of the diversity of races, but these would unite, to a large extent, in time, and then the Secretary of State for the Colonies would no longer be able to dictate to them. This Boer is evidently a man of a gloomy disposition, who will never accept any real fusion with the British whatever he may now say. He does not, in fact, try to hide his feelings, and resents bitterly the oath he was compelled to take. This, taking the oath, and Lord Milner's celebrated Capetown speech, are the chief matters which have given offence lately. It seems to me that the oath was a mistake: the alternate declaration which the Boers were willing to take would, in my opinion, have been preferable, and more binding than a forced oath.

In speaking of the taxes in the Transvaal under Kruger, No. IV. observed that the Republican Government was not a good one, because so many of its servants were, by reason of their want of education inefficient, and no doubt there was nepotism; but these were faults which could and would have been gradually remedied. In any case, the Government of Cape Colony was far worse, Rhodes' influence, which was absolutely supreme there, having encouraged corruption throughout the body politic. The Orange Free State was by far the best governed of the lot; then came Natal, then the Transvaal, and the Cape was the worst of all.

A Cape Englishman on board gave it as his opinion that the only thing to do was to give all posts to Englishmen, and to make the Dutch realise that they are under the English now. It is necessary to compel the Dutch to feel that they had to respect the English, and that only through the latter's favour could they hope for anything. This remark did not meet with general acceptance, but it is apparently the feeling of the low-caste Britisher at the Cape, and it must do much harm, because the Dutch will not submit to anything of the kind, nor is it likely or reasonable that they should do so. The Dutch on board are certainly, man for man, superior in force of character and self-reliance to the British passengers, and probably also in natural ability to the colonials. The Boers, I gathered, did not even approve of the Cape farmers who settled in the Transvaal after Majuba, but boycotted and bullied them so much that many of them returned south after a time.

Commercial probity does not seem to be high in South Africa, secret commissions being universal. Any firm resolutely refusing to adopt this custom would in the end prosper; at least that seems to be the general idea.

The Italians have three little ports south of Gardufui, which the skipper says are difficult to get in and out of. The Somalis in the neighbourhood are treacherous, proud, and turbulent, and the Governor and his guard are really prisoners on the forts which they have built. The country near the sea is barren, but after getting over the first range of hills it becomes green, and the Somalis have large herds of cattle, in which an extensive export trade is carried on. The population near the ports is very mixed, and for ages, Indians have traded and lived there, where, as all down the coast, they are the best business men. The Natal Government seem to be very foolish in not encouraging Indians to settle in the colony, it being evident that they are the best pioneers for all East Africa. Ships are now supplied with excellent vegetables, from the Italian ports, which are grown on the mountains, some distance away.

Beira was our next port. The harbour is at the corner of a large but very shallow bay. The town lies on Portuguese territory, and its prosperity depends on the Beira-Mashonaland railway which runs to Salisbury, but for many miles through Portuguese territory. Salisbury is 5,000 feet above the sea-level. A river runs out near the town, and the bay is a dirty light green colour, due, no doubt, to its shallowness. Prices are high at Beira. A bottle of beer costs 2s. 6d., and the charge to be taken on shore is 3s., against 1s. elsewhere. White men, apparently Italians, come out with the boats, but they only boss, black men rowing. Beira is under the influence of the Chartered Company, and may be taken as the commencement of British South Africa and British South African prices. It is built on a sand bank, and the streets are of the same material, along which carriage traffic is not practicable; the footpaths are cemented. The Chartered Company has laid light rails along the principal streets, and charge so much a year for people to run their own trolleys on them. Negroes supply the tractive force. There are many respectable English and Italian stores, as Rhodesia is supplied from Beira. A number of sportsmen also visit the place; buffalo are plentiful, and there are also lions, deer, and other game. The houses are, at present, more or less temporary, built of corrugated iron, but are being replaced by permanent structures. The railway connects Beira with all places in South Africa, but the Portuguese have so far not established telegraphic communication, even with Chinde.

I found that one of the young men on board, apparently a mining engineer by profession, had been in the Imperial Yeomanry for eighteen months, serving in South Africa. He holds the most ultra-gloomy view of our army, so much so, that he avoided conversation on the subject. He was more inclined to cry than to laugh at an institution which he thought could never be reformed, and was at present chiefly of use as a pastime for "Society." He had not received the pay due to him, and many of his *confrères* had written to him for small loans. From his account, the discipline of the Imperial Yeomanry left much to be desired. The men used to forge their officers' names to get cases of liquor, and treated the matter as a joke, the officers not daring to take serious notice of their conduct.

A small port in Portuguese territory was pointed out to me as two hundred miles from Madagascar and a hundred miles from the boundaries of the Transvaal, where one of the passengers was asked to land rifles during the war.

No. V. appears to be much exercised in regard to the

education question. He says that at the time of the treaty the Dutch were told that their language would be taught in the schools, but that in spite of this promise it is only taught for a few minutes daily as a Scripture lesson. The ladies who were sent out as teachers do not know Dutch, and he thinks—though this may be prejudice—that little care was observed in selecting them. Owing to poverty, he thinks that, for a time at least, many Boer children will be sent to the Government schools, but that where possible Dutch schools will be started, and that those who can afford it will send their sons to Holland.

As we approached Delagoa Bay the temperature fell and the nights became cool. Delagoa Bay is said to be the only port on the east coast which can be entered in all weathers. At Durban there is a bar which cannot always be passed, and then passengers have to be slung over the ship's side in a basket.

There was an instance last night of the touchy feeling everywhere prevalent, a row being with some difficulty avoided. A high judicial officer on board expressed strong hopes that the Dutch and English would combine, and he stated that inter-marriages still took place. He denies the utter want of confidence which seems to me to be so prevalent on both sides, but he himself in the same conversation showed strong traces of it. He is, of course, quite superior to the folly exhibited by the lower-grade colonist, and I have no doubt whatever that he sincerely desires peace. Another war would, he said, be far more bitter than the last.

I did not go on shore at Lorenzo Marques, as we only stayed a few hours—during the hottest part of the day. There were thirty large sailing-ships and ten steamers in the harbour, the former mostly laden with Baltic timber, two of the latter with cattle, mules, and asses from Europe and North Africa. The town, which is by far the busiest we have yet visited, lies on the flat ground to the right of the harbour, and extends to a pretty green hill on which there are new buildings looking much like an Indian hill station, huts and barracks appearing amongst plenty of trees. We took on board many deck passengers, who embarked with huge boxes at the last moment. The boatmen are chiefly Greeks and Italians, and the passengers come on board as late as possible, it is said, to avoid having their enormous boxes measured. Although it is reported to be hot on shore, the sun has evidently, as we have come further south, lost most of its power; on leaving port we found it quite cool and pleasant.

The ship was overcrowded when we arrived at Delagoa Bay, and we were now worse owing to more passengers having been put on board. Some were refused, we understand, despite the protests of the agent, whose interest lies in getting commission on the passage money. The unfortunate officers have been turned out of their cabins, and the state of affairs was simply appalling, and might easily lead to an outbreak of epidemic disease.

A German, in speaking of one of the passengers, said that Huguenot Boers still look on Roman Catholics as followers of Antichrist, and would rather fraternise with Jews than with them. He thinks that this intolerant spirit, which is especially strong in the women, who have most influence on the children, does not augur well for peace in the Transvaal. The women never seem to be able to forget an injury. He said that when the raid occurred the women in many cases drove out the men, who, not looking on the matter as serious, were in no hurry to go on commando. Similarly he said that the women in the concentration camps kept up a steady correspondence with the men outside, saying that they were all right and the struggle should on no account be given up. The statement often made that the Boers were brutal men to let their wives and children suffer for their obstinacy was quite erroneous; in fact, a burgher was often more afraid to face his wife than the enemy, and so kept on at the war.

An official of the Johannesburg Chamber of Mines concerned immediately with the labour question, who came on board at Delagoa Bay, admits that the unwillingness of the Kaffirs to return to work is a very serious matter. He said that there are seven thousand Europeans employed in the Transvaal in the mines who work on Trade Union principles. It was through their persistency that the seven hundred Imperial Yeomen, who were tried, were got rid of; not a single one now remains. He is in favour of exhausting all efforts to get what labour is required from Africa, but Exeter Hall—stupidly, he thinks—stands in the way of any compulsion, direct or indirect, being employed. Mr. Chamberlain insists on South Africa being kept as a preserve for the British, in consideration of the two hundred millions of pounds spent on the war, and Lord Milner has to fall in with this view. The latter is clever and absolutely straight, working with might and main for any cause he has espoused, but always on the square. The Chamber has a man in China looking into the Chinese immigration question, but Easterns will only be resorted to in the last extremity, on account of the strong opposition which would be evoked by such a measure. The whole of South Africa is very expensive, and Delagoa Bay the dearest place of all. Government is now building houses for their servants at Johannesburg, and the land companies are about to do the same, he believes. He is of opinion that the British at home do not feel their taxation, and could easily bear a great deal more. The Boers and English, he thinks, will easily agree in future, as the war has caused them to respect each other. The Cape Dutch are likely to be the coming trouble, "as they are all rebels"; they are "those that agitate, but never fought." At present 150,000 natives are wanted for the mines, and only 5,000 or so a month are coming in, against which about 2,000 leave. The Chamber of Mines is said to be spending £20,000 a month to overcome the labour difficulty. He thinks that Delagoa Bay is the best port for Johannesburg, but the Portuguese are always having holidays, when the railways are closed for goods traffic. The mine-owners, however, favour Delagoa Bay, as its existence tends to keep Durban and Capetown in order as ports. He frequently travels up and down the coast, and says that the boats are always equally crowded. Since the war has commenced the line must have paid immensely, and it is curious that there is no English opposition.

CHAPTER III

Landing at Durban—Race and labour questions—Natal colonists—Kaffirs—Lack of manufactures—Agriculture and horticulture in a very backward state—Wealth of the colony of Natal mostly due to wars—Benefit derived by Durban from the Transvaal gold discoveries—Skilled labour mostly white, but manual labour almost entirely done by blacks—Difficulty in obtaining a passport for Indian servant to proceed to the Transvaal—Food supply of the colony mostly imported.

WE were so far in luck, on reaching Durban, that the sea was calm, but we arrived at the outer harbour about 6.30 p.m., and the Health Officer does not come on board ship after 6 p.m., so that we had to wait outside all night. In the morning the pilot and Health Officer came on board, and the ship was moved into the inner harbour, which was fortunate, as the sea was beginning to get up. The day was hot, and the arrangements for landing baggage bad. It took me till six in the evening to get my cabin baggage to the hotel at which I was staying. It was whilst I was kept waiting for my own baggage that I had my first experience as to how natives of India were treated in Natal. A Multani, who had during the voyage fraternised with my servant, asked me to interpret for him to the immigration officer on board, who would not give him the landing ticket, without which he could not go on shore. On inquiry I found that he could not land because he had no permit, issued by the Natal Government, authorising him to come on shore. He had, when in Aden, entered into an agreement with an Indian firm in Johannesburg to join it, and had been furnished with a certificate from the office of the Supervisor of Asiatics, Johannesburg, addressed to th

British Resident at Aden, stating that the bearer, Kimadrai, had permission to proceed from Aden to Johannesburg, and asking that the necessary authority might be issued. This certificate was endorsed "Permitted to proceed," and signed by the officiating Political Resident at Aden. The Natal Government refused to recognise this document, but would have allowed him to proceed if he paid £10, to be returned to him at Johannesburg. He had only £4 with him, and was unable to do so. Had he been able to write any European foreign language, Italian or Modern Greek for instance, he would have been allowed to land, but Urdu, the general language of India, which he could write, was not sufficient. This preference to foreigners seems to me to be iniquitous, and the present regulations, which have been in force for less than three years to need change. The immigration officer appeared to see the injustice which was being inflicted, and suggested that perhaps the Multani would be allowed to land at East London, which the ship would reach within the next ten days. He, however, intimated that the Cape Government had a stronger Act coming into force shortly. There was nothing for it but to take the man's permit back to the ship and to interview the captain, who consented to allow the man to go on to East London. The ship's agents—Germans, of course—were mirthful as to the advantages of being a subject of the British Empire. If the man had been a Frenchman or an Italian no difficulties would have been raised.

At the dock all ordinary manual labour is done by coloured men (Indians and others), white men supervising. Whilst waiting to leave the ship the wife of a very decent Cape farmer entered into conversation with me. She had emigrated in 1879, and married a colonial. Neither she nor her husband are very well educated, but they are well-to-do. They have been home, and do not seem to have much fancied England, partly, no doubt, on account of the wet summer. They are not likely to repeat the visit. She observed that they were much surprised and a good deal pained to find as many Boers in England as at the Cape—

alluding to the opinions expressed by people they had met. On my suggesting that the income tax had possibly some effect on her English friends, she replied, "That is exactly what my husband says, but all the same we did not like it, and it was not pleasant to hear the talk we did." My suggestion was that they would find it necessary to get on with the Dutch. "Yes," she said, "but I am afraid it will be a very slow process. The feeling at present is terrible. During the war our neighbours, Dutch, the nearest fourteen miles away, were civil and apparently loyal. Since the war they are extraordinarily bitter, and I see no hope of this feeling changing." She had no experience of the feelings of the loyalists, but there was absolutely no doubt as to the dreadful effect the war had exercised on the tempers of the Dutch, and she seemed to look forward to the future with some dread. She was even doubtful whether it would not have been better to have accepted a Republic separate from England, and to have let the Dutch and colonists settle their own differences. She believed that such a solution was slowly coming, and that it might have a healing effect. Her husband never took any part in politics, though at election times he votes with the Progressives, and he finds even this to be a somewhat unpleasant duty.

At the hotel I had a talk with a Johannesburg man, who was on his way home. He said that Mr. Chamberlain was making sugary speeches, and that he has practically told the mine-owners that they can fix their own taxation. His own view is that the situation in Cape Colony is most serious. In his opinion almost all of the inhabitants of that colony are rebels. So far as the treatment of native races is concerned, he preferred the Bond policy. Natives should be kindly treated, but they should be kept in their place. What he really means is that all coloured men should do the whole manual labour of the country, but that under no circumstances should they be permitted to trade or rise above the position of unskilled labourers. The white men, however vicious, should do the supervision, and accumulate the profit. Under laws designed to secure such a state of affairs it is evident that fair treatment of natives can never be insured. Self-interest combined with all the power will prevent that.

The newspapers have an exaggerated account of the accident to our ship, as well as remarks, not too strong, on the subject of overcrowding. Mr. Chamberlain's speeches and the excessive demands of the Boers, more especially in regard to a general amnesty, also came in for comment. Another burning question is the bricklayers' strike; the men decline to accept 16s. a day, or even a maximum of 17s. My servant tells me that there are Madrasses in great numbers in the place, and that they seem to be permanently settling down. They are not allowed to be out after 9 p.m., but that Goanese—he himself being a Goa man—are not molested.

My Johannesburg friend tells me that the work in the mines is really very hard, that the men are hunted by white overseers, and that they never get ten minutes' rest, except during dinner hour. He had found that much worse labour was better paid in the Dutch Indies, and had come to the conclusion that 1s. 6d. a day was not enough. The mine-owners had, however, tried to reduce this wage, and every one I spoke to averred that higher wages could not be paid. They, however, admitted that high dividends had been the result of the low wages, which had led to the present labour difficulty. The Chamber of Mines seems at present to be angling for the importation of Chinese at rates of wages which will speedily have to be raised when John Chinaman grasps the situation.

It is admitted on all hands that the Durban people have made no end of money during the last three years, the war being practically the very best thing that could have happened to them. The same was the case during the Zulu war. Between the two wars the town languished, and the same thing will happen again. The reason seems to be dear labour—white labour and the restriction on coloured men's enterprise. Even in this hot place the roofs of the houses are still generally of sheet iron, whilst there is tile earth in abundance. Portland cement, at 15s. a barrel, is in general use, though lime could be had in abundance if labour was cheaper. Everywhere there is a pronounced air of *laissez-faire*, no proper arrangements, no tidiness, and no order. Hay and timber are stacked any way on the quays and elsewhere in the town; still the place seems to be fairly clean, and without smell.

Natal has a responsible Government, the legislature consisting of a House of Assembly, thirty-nine strong, and a Council nominated by the Crown. The Governor is permitted to interfere so far as native questions are concerned. The Governor is said to be disliked owing to his being supposed to interfere in political matters, and the Premier is very unpopular outside Pietermaritzburg, where his interests lie. The Ministry is at present in a majority of one. The only burning question before the Legislature just now is the proposal to double the present railway line to Johannesburg, which has gradients of one in thirty, and curves of three hundred, the counter proposal being a new line to the right of the present one, which would miss the range of hills that has to be negotiated up and down to Pietermaritzburg.

An Englishman eight years out, who is employed in sugar works fifty miles down the coast, gave me his views on the labour question. This industry depends entirely on Indian labour, Madrasis being preferred, and those interested are much concerned at the possibility of the Indian Government stopping emigration, as the sugar works could not be carried on without it. The town, on the other hand, objects to what is called undesirable immigrants. It is clear to me that though all here defend their treatment of the Indians, they know and feel that they have a bad case, and that some plain speaking on the part of the Indian Government would do much good. The Natalians are also touchy, and were not pleased when I told them of our having to get permits or passports for South Africa, though such are not required in France or Germany. The one hundred and fifty Indians who came on the ship with me from Zanzibar were, I heard, refused entry at Durban, and went on to East London. For some reason or other between four hundred and five hundred English, Scotch, and Irish had also been refused permission to land. My friend, who is interested in sugar, complains not only of dear labour, but of the intense conservatism of the Natal people. He thinks that both lime and tiles could be easily made locally, but he says that you would have to "oil the wheels" in all directions to get them taken up. He added that, under the present semi-military *régime*, Government moved so slowly that nothing could be got through. Free Local Government, he felt sure, must soon come, even in the Transvaal, where you could, under the Kruger administration, get business through in two or three hours that now takes four or five months. My friend is an ultra-Britisher, I should say, but we kept off all burning questions. He chatted away on local questions, in which he had a personal interest.

The police notice-boards are covered with notifications regarding the present intricate pass regulations, which seem to me to cause much inconvenience, to stir up ill-feeling, and generally to cause more trouble than they can be worth. The notifications speak of "the two conquered Provinces," a phraseology which irritates the Boers, and probably does more harm than would a harsh law administered with tact and common sense. The Boers are obviously a very touchy people, and anything that hurts their pride rankles for ever. At least, those to whom I have spoken say they will accept accomplished facts, only on condition that the treaty is carried out both in letter and spirit, and that they are treated in all respects as the equals of Britishers. They will accept no inferior status, and even to hint at anything of the kind is at once to kindle their unquenchable hostility. Absolute equality shown in social intercourse would soon heal the sore; anything short of this will only nourish a hatred that centuries will not obliterate. Many colonials see this, but I doubt if the high-collared colonial youth does so.

On all sides repeated references are made to bribery and

corruption in Durban, which is said to have come in with the war. It is reported to be prevalent in the Customs and railways, in fact everywhere. No doubt there is much exaggeration, but there is probably a substratum of truth. At any rate there does not seem to be any hesitation in speaking on the subject, and rumour goes so far as to accuse the Durban merchants of bribing the Portuguese authorities at Lorenzo Marques to put obstacles in the way of transit through that port to the Transvaal—to my mind a wildly improbable story.

A Cape commercial man, whom I accidentally met, says that the Bond is by far the strongest political organisation in South Africa. He is retiring, but will continue to hold property in and return yearly to winter in South Africa. He does not like the thought of paying income tax. He admits that the colonists have an unfair way of looking at these matters; they underrate the sacrifices the British people make, whilst steadfast in avoiding their share of them. He was very indignant at what he represented as the haughty and insolent manners of the military in Cape Colony, whilst martial law was in force, and objected strongly to, what he called, Khaki Government. The loyal colonists, in fact, are quite as averse to Imperial rule as the Dutch. The Bond, my informant said, will certainly rule at the Cape, and probably in time all over South Africa. Mr. Hoffmeyer is extremely clever, my friend considers, and he is at the bottom of the Bond. Merriman is also clever. Sir G. Sprigg is very autocratic, and with the obstinacy of age upon him. The amount of trouble the merchants at the Cape were subjected to, during the war, was appalling, but they made corresponding gains. He thinks that it is not sufficiently recognised that the times were abnormal. A Natal firm, on whom we called, was against the free entry of Indians, who would monopolise the market gardening, and ruin the whites—at least, "so we think," he said.

My Cape friend, who had made his pile, said that Kruger was a terrible liar, but a wonderful man all the same. Rhodes, he added, had also done a lot of good, but also a lot of harm. He did not like Rhodes' methods, many of the agents he employed were disreputable, for the reason that no self-respecting man would have done the work required. He is of opinion that if England was hard pressed elsewhere, the Boers would again fight for independence, otherwise the danger is small, provided they are carefully handled and not worried. One of the points in respect to the Khaki Government that my friend laid great stress on was the treatment people received during the war, which he said was very bad, and had never been truthfully described. As an instance, he said that at one place a farmer had all his farm horses impressed, six being kept exclusively for the colonel's wife to drive about with. He speaks well of Tommy Atkins, but does not seem to have a high opinion of the average British officer, who, he says, governs harshly where civilians are concerned, and will never, under any circumstances, take the smallest responsibility. As regards the harshness and overbearing manner of the British officer, the opinion given is, word for word, what the Dutch and Germans say, but they are naturally prejudiced, and their views did not impress me much. My present informant is, however, an out-and-out Englishman. He is also discriminating, and mentioned an old naval captain, who held a position of authority, as being very popular. On his office a large placard was suspended with the legend, "No red tape here." This naval gentleman's fame had reached me through other sources, as he was talked about on board ship.

Natal seems to be seething with burning race and labour questions. There are violently abusive and utterly unjustifiable letters in the Durban newspapers about letting Indians into the country to work on tea and sugar plantations, which are protected by heavy import duties. Indians, in general, are spoken of as "paupers, drunkards, thieves, and murderers, these being their leading characteristics even in India itself." It is on this kind of pabulum that the enlightened voters of Natal, in whose hands the government of the colony lies, are fed. The colony, it may be mentioned, has already more British Indians than white people in it. It seems to me that India ought to have some kind of resident and accredited labour agent, whose duty it would be to watch over the interests of Indian immigrants. The market place is half full of Indians, white and black stalls alternating, and even in the former Indians are employed as assistants. In a white fruiterer's stall a smart little Bombay man was employed at £6 a month.

The Natal colonist is, as a rule, a tallish, square-shouldered and nice-looking man, without any of the roughness observable in colder colonies. He is generally clean and well dressed, and of a gentlemanly appearance, largely, probably, owing to the rough, hard work being done either by Kaffirs or Indians. He moves slowly and seems to be wanting in energy, at least that is the only conclusion that can be drawn from the fact that none of the gardens are tidy, and the bicycles are rusty and appear never to be cleaned. But vehicles which require exertion are not used so much as rickshaws drawn by Zulus in most fantastic costumes, usually with a pair of cattle horns on their heads and a big plume of feathers. On meeting them suddenly in the street, it is not easy to tell whether you are facing a man or some kind of strange South African beast. The youths seem to affect dark clothes—black coats for choice—and straw hats. Pretty buttonhole flowers are almost universal. Turning to business, neither tiles nor lime is manufactured. The walls of the houses are thin and badly built. All the butter is imported, and there is practically no fresh milk, enormous quantities of tinned milk being imported. There seems, in fact, to be an entire absence of enterprise and energy. Meat is largely imported and kept in cold storage, and is never, in my own experience nor from what I can hear, fit to eat. The climate is excellent, particularly in respect to fruit-growing, but none of the fruit seems to be good, and what is exposed for sale looks stale and bad. No effort is made to properly cultivate mangoes or any other kind of fruit. It is too much trouble for the whites, and the more industrious races are not allowed to come in and do it for them. How is such a country to progress? It seems to me that under its present conditions progress is not possible, and that unless a radical change is made it will not support more than a handful of white people, unless a succession of wars brings grist to the mill in the future, as has been the case in the past. Wars have, in fact, hitherto been the chief means of subsistence of the colony, and the source of most of its wealth.

Durban has also profited by the imports which have poured into the Transvaal since the discovery of gold there. The hotel in which I am living has been in course of being built, and never finished during the last four years. Every ten steps one comes across half-finished rooms or staircases and balconies, and everywhere building refuse is left lying about. So far I have only seen one white carpenter at work, and he had, of course, a Kaffir assistant, for a white man has always a black man in attendance. When the white man goes home he leaves his bag of tools behind him, so that they could very easily be stolen. It is an easy-going, happy-go-lucky kind of life, but not an unpleasant one, in so good a climate, so long as it lasts, and England will pay for the wars that will be periodically provided by the colonists. The roads are turned into warehouses by the merchants, which does not look nice, but must be convenient and economical for the business men. Whether this practice is officially allowed, or tips come in, I cannot say, but Gardiner Street, at the bottom of which is the Marine Hotel, the Esplanade, and the inner harbour, are lined on both sides with corrugated iron and cases which have been lying there for days. There is, however, little traffic, except rickshaws and an occasional dray. The only manual labour done by whites seems to be shop-keeping and such work as bricklaying and carpentering. In the hotel Madrasis do the waiting, the cleaning and sweeping, and one white woman gives out the towels and makes the beds. The hotel washing is done by three Madrasis and three Kaffirs, who get £20 a month amongst them and free board and lodging. Of this remuneration the Madrasis take double the amount the Kaffirs get. A tradesman hailing from Edinburgh told me that Durban was the best kept town in South Africa, chiefly because it was mainly peopled by Scotch, who appreciate good government and insist on getting what they pay for. The fact that there were no Dutch was also an advantage. The water supply, coming from three different sources, was good.

A pass, both for myself and my Indian servant, to visit the Transvaal was necessary. It took me some time to get to the pass-granting official, who made no difficulty about myself, but said that, as my servant was a native of India, an order from the Supervisor of Asiatics at Pretoria was necessary, and this would take ten days to obtain. The servant can, however, go to Pietermaritzburg with me, and I will try to obtain his pass from that place. It does not seem to be obvious why, when Pretoria is only twenty-four hours distant, it should be necessary to take ten days to obtain a permit; it also seems to be impolitic in the face of the irritation which exists against the present semi-military *régime*. By the way, foreigners applying for a pass have to produce a certificate from the Consul of the country to which they belong. Indians have to obtain an order from the Supervisor of Asiatics at Pretoria. If Indians are to be treated as foreigners, an Indian immigration agent, under the control of the Indian Government, seems to be a necessity, as otherwise they have no one to protect them, whilst foreigners will be supported by their Consul.

It is noticeable that the postmen, telegraph boys, car conductors, and ticket-collectors at the railway stations are all white, but that every kind of manual labour, except the trades, which are rigorously preserved for and by them, is done either by Indians or Kaffirs. It is a matter of easy *versus* hard work, as the whites keep even small street booths, selling to rickshaw men and the like. In fact, they will follow the lowest kind of occupation, provided only that it is easy and profitable.

There was a tremendous wind, with clouds of dust, which cut short my journey outside. The bay was very rough, and I congratulated myself that we had good weather when we landed. Port Elizabeth and East London are said to be as bad ports as Durban, depending entirely on the weather. Cargo receives fearful treatment in bad weather, and all ports are now so jammed with goods that, with this plethora of supplies and the everlasting labour troubles, it takes a ship fourteen days to a month to unload.

A Scotchman who has been here for one-and-a-half years says that the Scotch and Dutch ought to amalgamate to some extent, the former being in many ways more like the Dutch than the English. He says that every one who comes here is struck, as I am, with the general *laissez-faire* all round, and the fact that these colonies are a long way from self-supporting, even in the matter of food. Besides importing meat (which, from bad cooking, is usually almost uneatable) and practically all the milk and butter used, they also largely import flour. Every one tells me that no white man will touch hard manual labour on any terms whatever. To such an extent is this country now inhabited by coloured people, that a bank manager asked me if there were as many whites in Bombay as in Durban. The Natalians seem, in fact, to compare their colony more with India than with Great Britain. They, however, assert that, in respect to going easily, things at the Cape are worse, as *there* it is always, "Don't be in a hurry." My friend says that there are far more Dutch than English in South Africa, and that it is hopeless to expect British agricultural immigration. The most likely plan, he thinks, is to try to educate the young Dutch, who, he says, have good heads, to ideas of progress. But education would not unlikely lead with them, as it has done in the case of other people, to towns and theatres. At present they hate both, and love their farms. My Scotch friend showed me a newspaper article reviewing Rider Haggard's "Rural England," which seems to deal very sensibly with the subject.

At dinner a thin, pale Englishman sat beside me. He is a fruit-grower, living only fourteen miles from Spion Kop. He has been out fourteen years, and quite admits that the colony has its bad, as well as its good, side. He stuck to his farm throughout the war, and was never molested, though he was told that his property would be destroyed if he moved away. He would rather have been looted by the Boers than by the Imperial troops, as the former, being farmers, sympathise with their class. They would never ruin orchards and plantations, as the British did, in many places close to him. He had never been outside Natal. He heard the guns and volleys continually, and quite plainly, but never went to see the fighting. I agreed with him that it was, after all, more pleasant to see one smiling farm than ten burnt ones, even with a battlefield thrown in. He liked the Boers, and had always got on well with them. He hoped and trusted that the Home authorities would not interfere in native questions, which the Boers understood far better than we had ever done, and he thought that any interference would bring about a republic, whilst he confessed that he was not himself certain whether, after all, such a Government would not be the best in the conditions brought about by the war. He has always employed Kaffirs, but is going to change to Indians, for whom he has applied to the Government Immigration Department for the last twelve months, but so far has not got any, the demand being so great. Many of his neighbours employed Indians, as the Kaffirs are irregular and lazy. Like every one here, he evidently approves of Indians being either sent back to India at the end of their five years or re-indentured. He does not want to see them as thriving neighbours.

Land has become very expensive in Durban; a site 100 feet by 50 feet, with a frontage of 50 feet was lately sold for £12,000. The cost of buildings is, no doubt, proportionately high. There is some truth in the newspaper report regarding the unpopularity of Australians, but the main reason of the animus against them seems to be that a number of carpenters and masons came over who are good workmen but also born agitators. Labour is not well organised in Natal, and has no funds. A New Zealand friend, who has never been to Europe, seems to like Durban fairly well. He says the Natal people are rather odd and touchy, and very angry if you do not praise Durban. They are very conservative in regard to business, and will often stick to an old house long after they can do better elsewhere. If they once take you up, you are safe. The great aim of Durban is to be the port for the Transvaal. The Natalians prefer to be thought immigrants rather than born in the country, which is a great pity, and argues a want of grit.

After despatching a telegram, the shops along the north side of West Street engaged my attention. They are mostly clothing shops, or fruiterers', kept by Indians—all neat and clean, if small. They have also spread east of Grey Street, and there is one shop, where Indian curios are sold, on the south side of the street. The other shops are kept by white people, with "ladies" and "gentlemen" to serve, and Kaffirs occasionally, but seldom Indians, to clean and help. One meets many respectable Indians in the streets, generally Bombay men, who are evidently traders, as distinct from the coolies who mostly come from Madras, but a few from Calcutta.

A lady who has been in the country for many years has been telling me, at the hotel during meals, the old story as to the dearth of servants. Apparently the well-to-do employ white servant girls, when they can get them, some of these being colonials. Since the war all get high wages. The Indian coolies employed on gardens, she says, are slaves, and nothing more. They are bound for five years, at what she evidently considers to be miserable wages, and can be lent out to other masters. Some are well treated, and some very much the reverse. The masters can, in point of fact, inflict any punishment they think fit, short of murder, and the coolies are practically helpless. A lot of them, men and women, driven along like a pack of sheep, by a native with a stick, passed me on the road.

At a dinner party I met a roving Englishman who had been in most places, and amongst his other avocations had many years ago driven a cab in New York. This employment at that time he described as robbery, pure and simple, and he fell in with the usual custom, looting any one who fell into his hands, to the best of his ability, and squaring the police. Under Mr. Kruger and his corrupt oligarchy he would have had a bad time of it, but as it was, he quickly got dollars together and left off cab-driving. During dinner the casual life of the South African colonies, its Kaffir servants, who are equally casual, and its many inconveniences, came up for discussion, and it was agreed that after all "money could be made, which was the only thing one came out here for." There was no attempt at shirking this candid avowal, and it was made in a manner very depressing to an unpatriotic Briton, who does not put wealth as the end of all existence. I ventured to suggest, that perhaps present comfort should be taken into account, and that there were various ways of making money, some of which fail, after a life of worry.

The generally accepted opinion was, however, that Durban was full of wealth, some of which was amassed in ways that were dark, but that no questions were asked, so long as the money was there, and that the very purpose for which every one came to Durban was to make money as fast as possible and then to leave. One young man dissented, and even took the position that it was possible to be happy without being rich, more especially if the riches were ill-gotten. He also thought that the Indians were not fairly treated, but said that all the same they were making money, and more and more exercising the power which wealth was bound to give them. On one point all were agreed, which was that though the European merchants did not like coloured men, they would give the Indians better and longer credit than they would to dealers of their own race. In some few cases colonial-born Indians are being employed as clerks, and it is noticeable that New Zealanders who have learnt to respect the Maoris, do not share the prevalent feeling against Indians. Yankees are, of course, strongly prejudiced and hot on the American negro difficulty, but admit that the position of the latter must improve as they increase in numbers and education, and that President Roosevelt is doing his duty as he understands it. Anyway, in one house, a chummery of three bachelors, I found three Kaffir servants doing all the work, and cheerful and desirous to please. Whiskies and sodas, with immense quantities of tea, form the chief drinks here. Men in offices appear all to go out to drink tea at 11 a.m. and again at 4 p.m. They have an hour for lunch besides. Both offices and shops close punctually at 5 p.m.

CHAPTER IV

Roman Catholic cathedral—Protector of Immigrants—Durban peculiarities—Scarcity of labour—Objection of whites to do hard manual labour—Native question constantly alluded to, but never defined—Conversations with Indians—Berea—Colonial criticisms of Rhodes and Kitchener—Divine service—Demeanour of military officers—Numbers of whites, Indians and Kaffirs—Tramways in Durban—New Zealanders and Australians—Commercial standing of Indians—All progress in horticulture due to Indians—An American's opinion of the colonists.

THE native part of the town of Durban is rather miserable and untidy, and Indians of the coolie class are a dirty-looking lot dressed in any kind of old European clothes. It is a pity that they do not stick to their native costume. They are practically freed from the trammels of caste, but unfortunately have found nothing to take its place, and to put some restraint on the suiting of their individual tastes in the matter of manners and customs, without reference to the comfort or views of their neighbours. The same thing has frequently been noticed in the case of Europeans and Americans when first settling in places not previously inhabited.

Near the native town, however, I saw a large cathedral with handsome marble columns, on each side of the nave being built. My immediate exclamation was that the building probably belonged to the Roman Catholics, for it is not, I fear, very much the custom for the Church of England to erect a cathedral, or even a large church, in the slums of such places as Durban. My surmise was correct, and it seems to me that in such towns as these only Roman Catholic padres are worthy of their calling. Church of England parsons, well-dressed, clean, and gentlemanly-looking, abound, but I should as soon expect to see St. Paul as any one of these divines, in the crowded slums of an Eastern city. The Roman Catholics, on the other hand, appear not only to seek, but to find, the poor and rejected ones of this world. Close by the cathedral, for which Marseilles tiles were being collected, was a large cemetery, the condition of which was not creditable to a town like Durban. It is true that the soil is sandy, but the whole place is neglected and a sorry sight to look on. Next door there was a still more neglected cemetery, evidently set apart for poor Indians. Plague patients, of which there are a few, are buried at sea, but so near the harbour, that it does not seem to be a good plan.

The Protector of Immigrants has rather a nice office, but does not appear to be in a hurry to see the persons for whose benefit his services are retained; at least I saw thirty or forty coolies, men and women, at the door of the office, awaiting the leisure of this official, who was busy reading the newspaper. The Protector should be an Indian civilian of good standing, and should be well paid. The employers of the immigrants have to pay the cost of the office and the charges for importing the coolies; if these are tolerably heavy it is possible that Indians may receive more consideration than they do at present. The Natalians seem to think that Anglo-Indian officials have the same hatred and contempt for Indians, and would help to oppress them. They would speedily find themselves mistaken.

The rates and taxes in Durban are very low, due to the city having in its early days reserved some town lands which are valuable now. There are several lines of ships running direct to Durban, Clan, Harrison, Elliman, Newrie and others, and their average freight charges are 47½ shillings a ton, against 55 shillings by the Union mail line.

It appears that not a casting is made in Durban: they are all imported, as well as doors and windows. Carpenters get 17s. 6d. a day, whereas the pay of clerks who can write shorthand and typewrite is about £15 a month. It is commonly said that stationmasters, dockmen, and so on all round, have to be tipped, but that the higher Customs officials are all honest, and so are most of the municipal servants. Durban has good roads, which are kept fairly clean, usually by Indian sweepers of kinds. No coloured men are allowed in the streets after 9 p.m. without a pass signed by their master. This is said to be necessary to prevent fights among the Zulus, but the restriction is, of course, without any such justification, extended to Indians. The Durban people, however, themselves, very wisely, turn in at an early hour. The newspapers report that the Johannesburg people have already, since Mr. Chamberlain's speech, held a meeting to protest against the importation of either Indians or Chinese for work in the mines, or the other occupation in the Transvaal.

The *Rand Daily Mail* is rather violent on the subject, and demands the abolition of the appointment of Supervisor of Asiatics. It is strongly opposed to the present bureaucratic rule, and comments on what it styles the insolence shown by Government officials since the war. The appointment of an Indian police officer to be chief of the Johannesburg police is also, I see, strongly objected to. This newspaper states that the labour trouble is due to the rapacity of the mine-owners, who have, since the war, reduced the pay of the Kaffir miners, thinking that the new Government would help them to force the Kaffirs to work. As a fact, all over South Africa, wages have gone up enormously.

It is said that if better wages were offered European miners could be obtained; it is, however, exceedingly doubtful if this is the case. It is not a question of wages, but colour. British workmen might be promised and paid any wages (say £1 a day), but within a month of coming out they would cease to do hard manual labour themselves, and be bossing coloured men as they do now. This, so far as Natal is concerned, is the real difficulty, and the extraordinary thing is that no one seems to recognise it, and to encourage Indians being employed on all or any trade for which they are suited, whilst otherwise it is patent to every one that the work is not done at all. It is, in fact, a question between importing most things or manufacturing them in Natal by coloured labour. At present I can give no opinion, based on personal observation, in regard to the Transvaal, but there are large numbers of Kaffirs there, and white men will never, I feel certain, work alongside them in the same capacity. Reuter also wires that Mr. Chamberlain's speech has produced strong protests at home. The key of the position is, however, "White men will never do hard manual work where there are coloured races to do it for them." This aspect of the case I have never seen alluded to, or even hinted at, in the sheets and sheets written on the labour question. It is apparently thought not safe to mention it, for the real difficulty must be well known to some at least of the writers.

The railway goods-sheds seem to me to be well and carefully managed. White men do the tallying at various points along the sheds. Kaffirs carry the goods to the trucks, and Indians do the loading. The relative status of the three races is fairly well represented in this division of labour. The trucks, it may be mentioned, were all under cover. The goods consisted largely of deal planks and scantlings, made-up door frames and other kinds of building materials, and furniture and carriages. A small house, built of corrugated iron, consisting of six small rooms in one storey, and standing on a plot of ground 100 ft. by 40 ft., was pointed out to me as a fair example of the houses tenanted by clerks. It was bought two years ago for £1,300, and would now rent at £10 a month. The inmates were Britishers, who hoped to make money and return home. This tendency to leave the country is in favour of the Indians who remain permanently, in spite of the difficulties put in their way. Many Indians are making money, and slowly but surely improving their position even in Natal. This gradual rise in status seems to be the real reason of the unpopularity of the Indians, and the feeling would no doubt extend to Kaffirs if they were more intellectual, and were trade rivals of the whites.

The "native difficulty" is a subject which is constantly under discussion, but the precise meaning of the words no one can explain. It seems to refer to the Kaffirs becoming aware that their labour is really worth a good deal more than the two shillings a day they have been accustomed to get for it at the mines. The white man gets from five to ten times as much—ten to twenty shillings—and the newspapers, in commenting on the matter, frequently assert that in point of physique and efficiency for hard manual labour the Kaffirs are as good as the whites, whilst the Indians are not strong enough for work in the mines. The mine-owners are trying hard, and they will try harder, to make Government force the Kaffirs to work, not for a wage which they would be willing to accept, but for the sum which mine-owners and white people generally consider a sufficient wage for "the particular needs of Kaffirs," as the canting expression here runs. Direct slavery cannot be attempted, but indirect and unfair measures—sure to be resented—are aimed at. Hence the anticipated trouble and the talk of the coming native question, with the prospect of Boers and Britons combining to adopt any method, however drastic, to squash the blacks, and at the same time attract a few more millions towards South Africa.

Berea is the Malabar Hill, on a large scale, of Durban, and on my way thither I saw for the first time a really clean, well-dressed Bengali, evidently of a better caste than those I had previously met. He had stuck to his national dress, and had the appearance of a thoroughly respectable well-to-do Hindu. He was alone in rather a secluded place, attending to lamps which had been fixed where the road was under repair. On being spoken to in Hindustani, and asked if he did not come from Behar, he was rather amused, and said, "No, from near Calcutta." He had been in Natal for fourteen years, having come out with two others, who were still living here. They were Chatris by caste. He looked like a man of this caste, and had the usual string of beads round his neck. On being asked how he liked Durban, Hindu-like, he evaded the question and commenced a long philosophical discussion, the purport of which was, "That the place (Durban) was, of course, good. It had been made, as all other places were, by God, who made nothing ill. India and Natal were alike, the gifts of a good God, and there was nothing in them of which complaint could justly be made. It was not for him to grumble, but to bear any troubles cheerfully. He might return to India some day, but he would prefer not attempting to fix a time, because if he said he should depart to-morrow, he might die to-night. Men and places are in the hands of God, and no one could predict what would happen." Asked if he liked the people of Natal, he at first attempted to parry the question by again referring to the country itself as being good. When informed that I was myself a stranger from India, and that there were matters which seemed to me to require amendment, he said that he did not like being called a "coolie," with an adjective before it, by every European in the place, no matter how low-born he might be, but that as this was the usual form of salutation, he was getting accustomed to it. He further observed that "God made us what we are, also you. I say no more, for what can I do? I read my *shastres* and do my work. God once swept the world over with water, and may do so again. We do not like being called offensive names." With "Ram, Ram," which much pleased and amused him, I departed, and climbed the rough and sandy hill in front of me, and soon found myself amongst nice large houses situated on its crest, which afforded most pleasant and extensive views over the town, harbour, shipping, bluff, and outer bay.

The remark previously made, that there were no tidy gardens in Natal, does not apply to the gardens attached to these houses, which were not only well kept, but large, and contained many fine trees. In one instance there was a clump of large bamboos, and the dwarf variety is used as a hedge. There were many mango trees, but the fruit was small. The electric light is everywhere being carried up the hillside, and must be very convenient.

There were many military officers about, some in uniform and others not so, but they seemed to keep entirely to themselves, never, so far as I have seen, speaking to a civilian. The reason for this demeanour is not known to me, but it was remarkable and unmistakable—they seemed all to know each other and no one else. They sat together, and kept aloof from every one else.

My American friend on the ship is still at Durban, and has gathered stores of information at the bars in the evening. The town *is* full, according to him, of very free drinking saloons, and the talk there seems to be characterised by extreme openness of speech—not always edifying. He was much astonished at the terms in which he heard Rhodes, and even Kitchener, spoken of; the language was such that he declined to repeat it. All these matters, he says, were talked about in the loudest voices, so that any one could hear; and the particular detractors of Rhodes were Rhodesians. I mention these accusations, not as having any weight in respect to the men criticised, but as showing what is now moving men's minds in South Africa.

On the following day, in a church near the town hall, I found fair singing and a decent service. The interior was decent also. The padre read a prayer before the sermon in the place of the fashionable "In the name of," etc. The bell was pulled by a native, as in India, and there were a few electric fans, but they were 18 ft. high, and not, I should say, very useful; on this day they were not at work. The seats were labelled, and so, I suppose, rented. Plates, not bags, were used for the collection, so the sheep and the goats could easily be separated. The congregation was almost entirely Scotch; hence, no doubt, this business-like precaution. The church was well filled, and there were as many men as women, if not more. All were decently and cleanly dressed, but the Sabbath garments were diverse, extending to a brown holland suit. The sermon—eighteen minutes long—was a fair one, and dealt with the desirability of accepting Dissenters as good Christian brethren in spite of their particular organisation on forms of worship. The congregation thoroughly enjoyed and joined in the 275th hymn. How far they applied it to themselves is doubtful, seeing that they are steeped in racial animosities. I wonder whether they really hope to be one people, in the next world, with coolies.

The influx of officers seems to be caused by the troopship *Manitoba* being due to leave for England to-morrow morning. The people in the hotel do not know what regiments are leaving; in fact, they show the indifference on such matters which prevails here. "The officers usually have private means, and their money is liked," was a remark made to me. I hazarded a few words to two young officers, but was answered in monosyllables, and they clearly showed that they conversed only with their own community. It is, of course, possible that they know that they are not very popular out here, and they may also think that they are unfairly depreciated and judged.

Natal is supposed to be *par excellence* the British colony of South Africa, but it seems to me that it ought to be considered rather a dependency of the type of India than a colony like Canada or Australia. It is obvious that the British people who come to settle are few. It is too hot to be a colony for Britishers, and those living here make no secret of their intention to return home as soon as they have made sufficient money. The men one meets are mostly young, and there is a deficiency of women, who are 20 per cent. at least below the men in number. The men live mostly in boarding-houses or chum together, the great expense of house rent being unfavourable for married life. The population is not likely to increase beyond the number the towns will support with a chance of making money.

There are said to have been 70,000 Europeans and colonials in Natal, mostly the former, of whom 30,000 lived in Durban, 20,000 in Maritzburg, and the rest in the smaller towns or in the country, mostly, however, in towns; but it is doubtful if there are now over 60,000. On the other hand, there are 50,000 British Indians, of whom 35,000 are free; that is to say, their indentures expired previous to

1897, when a special law, since increased in stringency, was passed to keep them from permanently settling in the country, and it is proposed to compel all indentured coolies to return to India when their time expires—to make, in fact, their indentures expire after they have relanded in India.

The Indians live mostly in towns, 15,000 being in Durban and 3,000 in Maritzburg. But in spite of all laws the number of Indians settling permanently in Natal is increasing. Many were born in the country. Just now I saw a very nice sort of baker's cart, with lamps, a good nag, and smart harness, with two well-dressed Madrasis in charge. The name on the cart was Indian. They are a saving race, and are likely eventually to enormously outnumber the whites, even if the latter succeed in their present attempt to use new-comers as beasts of burden only and to insist on their leaving when their indentures expire. This treatment the Indian Government can easily prevent, and they should certainly do so. Above these two races, in point of numbers, are the Zulus, who are said to be about a million strong, those in Zululand included. Some of the Zulus are being educated, and as they are a strong, plucky, muscular race, they will, when they realise their own strength, have to be reckoned with. The late war is said to have given them an idea of their own power. It seems to be certain that the coloured races will have a good deal to say, in Natal, in possibly the not very distant future. The folly, not to say the crime, of giving over the country to the selfish rule of a handful of money-making Europeans, with no real attempt to see that coloured races have a fair chance to improve their position, will not unlikely lead to serious consequences, and these will be the natural result of that want of forethought and courage which has led to the present condition of affairs. The state of things mentioned cannot be lost sight of in considering the relative position of Dutch and English in South Africa.

In the course of a walk I came across a brickfield, and at another place a lot of boys playing cricket, with a kerosene tin as a wicket. They were all Indians with the exception of one European boy, who was enjoying the game as much as the rest. The language spoken was bad English. Everywhere I met Indians and Kaffirs, mostly the former, and at least twenty coloured men to one white man. The Europeans were mostly riding, whilst many of the Indians were driving light carts, frequently with their women and children, it being Sunday.

An officer with whom I was able to get up a conversation entirely agreed with me in respect to the Indian question, and said that Durban was far the best place in South Africa because of the Indians. "Wait until you get up-country," he said, "and you will see the difference." He said it would be a perfect godsend if Natal were flooded with Indians rather than that they should be kept out. In speaking of the way the colonies have made and are making money out of the war, leaving the Old Country to pay the taxes, he remarked, "That is why so many of us out here are turning little Englanders." My friend is going home on leave after twelve months' service in South Africa. He was in India for six years, and was much struck, as I had been, with the resemblance of Durban to Bombay. He thinks the people in Natal are far better off than higher up country. He paid his Goanese cook £7 a month, and when he left, the man showed him a letter offering £15 a month for services as a cook in a second-class hotel in Johannesburg. So far as this officer is concerned the glamour of the Uitlander has departed, and when the colonists talk to him about their special loyalty he replies that he has not the smallest reason to doubt them, as it is under present circumstances their obvious interest to permit England to pay for wars of which they reap the profit.

Another day I had a pleasant walk on the ridge ending at the tramway terminus. The day was delightful; a cool breeze with clouds about, and the sun, even when out, no hotter than it is on a summer's day in London. The tramway-ticket man told me that he and most of the men employed by the tramway company were New Zealanders who had either stopped after the war or gone home and returned. There had, he said, been a large influx of

Australians, and he thought they liked the colony fairly well. They seem to have come in greater numbers than Britishers, owing to the long drought and hard times at the Antipodes. The top part of the Berea hill is still negotiated in horse-cars, three powerful Australians abreast, which take so much holding that a Kaffir is allowed to drive, the work, I suppose, being so hard that white men do not like it. By the way, in India I have often tried to ascertain whether the half-caste's dislike of manual labour is due to false pride or to laziness. I am now inclined to think that the latter is the more potent cause, as I find that in Natal white men will do any work, however loathsome, provided it is not physically hard or trying. They keep miserable little shops on the wayside, and sell liquor to negroes; they are butchers and bootblacks at the street corners. It is, in fact, one of their grievances that Indians are taking to wayside shops. One I saw to-day was far cleaner than the majority of those kept by the whites. The driver told me that the horses cost on an average about £35 each, and he thought the pair he was driving were worth £50 each.

The top of the ridge has beautiful trees along it, and the lane was full of greenery and wild flowers. There are not many birds except bulbuls. There were nice houses and well-kept gardens all along at intervals. In some of the houses there were Indian servants; in others, white women-servants in the house and Zulus outside. In the distance there were ranges and ranges of rounded hills, some with flat tops, and all green and fresh-looking, with patches of cultivation, mealies, and sugar-cane here and there, but apparently no regular settled agriculture like Europe or India. All over the nearer hills and valleys small corrugated iron houses were dotted about, and there were some on the roadside itself. I was told that these huts were inhabited by Indians, who owned them and the ground around. A few looked fairly comfortable, with blinds and chairs. The usual Indian love of animals was apparent; dogs, birds in cages, fowls, and the useful goat were plentiful. Plants in kerosene tins abounded, the marigold being well in evidence. Along the road were many carts carrying hides, often drawn by six mules, the drivers being nearly always Indians. What Natal would do without this industrious, long-suffering race it is difficult to say. According to my military friend, they are enormously missed in the Transvaal; and it is owing to them that Durban is the most desirable place, as a residence, he has seen in South Africa.

Finding a Madrasi mending a wire fence, I had a chat, and learnt that he had been in Natal for twenty-four years, always with one employer, whom he still served. He had been to India once in that time, and might go again. He did any kind of work, masonry included. His master owned several houses, and lived in one hard by. This Madrasi's pay was £3 a month and a bag of rice. He had a son who was a clerk in the railway office and got £3 2s. 6d. a month. All the houses near belonged to Indians, who took in washing or worked in the town. There were men calling themselves Brahmans in Natal, but he did not see how they could be real Brahmans, seeing that they had crossed the sea, and that they ate fish. How was he to tell? He had evidently no faith in them, though he still had all the instincts of a Hindu. But there were some high-caste Hindus from Calcutta and many well-to-do Bombay men in Durban, where several Indians were landholders. His master had given him a piece of land, but the papers had not been made out, and I suggested that it might be well to have them completed. There were schools with white teachers, attended by Indian children, of whom there is no lack; these schools were said to have been in existence for the last ten years. In the compound of one house I saw a large *shamiana*, and found that I had rightly divined that there had been a wedding there the preceding day. Indian trees and shrubs were plentiful, including, amongst others, plantains and loquats. I passed a pretty little churchyard, with quite an English-looking parsonage attached, but the church was made of iron, and not in very good repair.

A friend dined with me the previous evening, and warned me that the white people here were very touchy on the point of colour. The curfew rang out, whilst we were talking, at 9 p.m. The bell rings for five minutes, and from that time all coloured people must remain in their houses. My friend confirmed the statement I had previously heard, that, after all, Indians could get better and longer credit from bankers than white men. My permit from Pretoria for my Indian servant has been issued, so I am advised by wire. My servant says that permits are, he hears, not difficult to get, but that they take usually ten days to procure.

Three Indians, one Mohammedan, and two Parsees, educated men, had conversations with me as to the way British Indians are treated in Natal. They were all extremely moderate in their arguments, and fully understood the other side of the question. They had no wish to claim political equality with whites, but they did claim fair treatment and reasonable opportunities for the exercise of their energy and talents. They were convinced that there was no chance of such treatment being accorded unless the Indian Government insisted on it, and, failing to obtain satisfaction for their people, stopped emigration to Natal. Without the Indian immigrants Natal would soon become a desert. They had no doubt that the Viceroy of India was well disposed towards them, but after all he was subordinate to the Secretary of State, in whom they had no kind of confidence, and who, they said, would do anything to catch votes. How, argued they, could any man in his position, and dependent on white men's votes, be expected to do anything else? Even if a strong man like Mr. J. Chamberlain were in Lord George Hamilton's place it would not, they thought, make much difference. The Natal Government was no doubt very much against them, and it was, of course, self-governing; it could not, however, stand against a determined effort on the part of the Indian Government. The new colonies were, any way, not self-governing, and the English Government could see that there was fair play there for Indians, as for all British subjects. The fact is, they remarked, that Indians are now much worse off than under the Dutch. Kruger had harsh laws against Indians, but they were not enforced. Now the whites are clamouring for these laws to be enforced to the letter, and for Indians to be excluded. So far as Natal is concerned, it owes its existence to Indians; until they came there was not a pine-apple in the country, nor, in fact, anything but mealies. The Indians showed the whites how fruit should be grown, and, at the present time, they grow all the vegetables procurable in the market. Instead of abusing the Indians, why did not the white people do the work themselves? London, they heard, was full of white people who were in great want of work. If so, why not import them to cultivate the land? Why were not these people brought to do the work which, I must have seen, was everywhere done by Indians? And if white people would not do the hard work incidental to cultivating the ground, why should the Indians who did it be begrudged what they could earn? They inquired if I had noticed that Cape Colony, which had always been scoffing at Natal on account of coolie labour, was now itself trying to get the same, but, of course, on the indenture system, which is practically civilised slavery. The wages, 12s. a month to start with, and never more than £1, are inadequate; and the policy of forcing these people out of the country, which they have enriched by their labour, is grossly oppressive. Kaffirs, whose labour is less valuable, as they are less intelligent, get in Durban from 4s. to 7s. a day. Natal is called the garden colony. Who made it the garden colony? Until the Indians arrived not a cabbage was grown. The Protector of Immigrants seems to be an official appointed by the Colonial Government, who have lately sent a mission to India to try to arrange that the coolies' indentures shall expire in India, a point which it is hoped will not be conceded. The Mohammedan said that there were some Europeans who desired to be fair to the Indians, but they were few in number; and what could they do? He gratefully mentioned the names of the honoured few. Indian children were not admitted into Government schools, but the Indian community had established many private ones.

In a conversation with a firm of British merchants regarding taxation they said that the only tax they paid, except customs, was a licence tax, which was levied on wholesale and retail traders alike, and in their case amounted to £50 a year. They said that they did not think that there was any town in the world so rich as Durban, size being taken into account. Income taxpayers at home may note this fact : prices in shops seem to fluctuate and hotel bills are frequently reduced if charges are objected to. A Scotch carpenter whom I interviewed said that he had been in South Africa for several years, but only five months in Durban, which was hotter than he liked. He was working on a six-roomed house, which would be rented for £9 a month—a proceeding he looked on as amounting to robbery. He considered South Africa as a far better place than Scotland for a working man, as the men were much more their own masters. My view is that he might have added, the masters of the rest of the community. Though rents were high, wages were still higher in proportion, and in the Transvaal they were higher still, even if the extra expenses in that colony were taken into account. He travelled daily by tram—a fourpenny fare—and then went six miles by train to escape the high rents to which he objected. He said that many workmen were building their own houses on money loaned by building societies.

A gentleman from the Cape, whilst admitting that most things, including food, were imported into South Africa, said that good agricultural land was to be had in the northern parts of the Cape and that irrigation was not essential. Australians, however, who had stopped after the war, had all left Rhodesia after giving its agricultural capabilities a trial. Capetown, in his view, is the most important town in South Africa, and its harbour is being greatly improved. He thought that the South African League had made a great mistake in appointing Dr. Jim their president, the raid being too serious an error to be forgotten ; and he, not Rhodes, was, he believed, the real author of it. However, it had brought on the war, without which South Africa could never have gone ahead. There is no question that the war has made the port go ahead and grow rich. He thought diamonds a very proper subject for taxation. The climate of Capetown he thinks better than Durban. A professional Durban man, an Englishman by birth, confirmed my Mohammedan friend's statement that until the Indians came Natal had no vegetables. He thinks that the indentured coolies are greatly underpaid, and that it is not right to work them at a large profit and then turn them out of the country when their indentures have expired. It is not politic, he thinks, even for the white man's future.

People at Durban are getting nervous about plague. I was several times consulted about it, and warned those who spoke to me about the ill-treatment of natives, which is pretty sure to occur if there is a panic. There is no proper accommodation for Indians on the quarantine island in the harbour to which they are taken. The newspapers are getting plague on the brain, and I am anxious to get away as soon as possible, as there may be quarantine against Durban. Some Dundee coal was shown to me, which is largely sold to the shipping, and which the proprietors claim to be equal to the best Welsh ; an analysis sheet was produced proving that it was better. Be that as it may, it was delivered on board ship for 24s. 6d. a ton. Complaints as to the high railway freight—9s. a ton for 250 miles—were made, and the Government management of the dock and railways was animadverted on.

I met an old Yorkshireman, long domiciled in Australia, who frequently takes Durban on his way from Australia to England. His view regarding the causes of the war—and he was in Natal shortly before it commenced—are very pro-Boer. He admits that it is only lately that he could avow them in Australia, but that now many agree with him. The people in Durban are so immersed in money-making that there is little sociability, many people not even knowing the name of their next-door neighbour. The banks keep short hours, closing at 2 p.m., except on Saturdays, when they close at 1 p.m. At present the nights are stuffy and hot, but it always gets cool towards morning. Some Bombay Mohammedans poured out their grievances to me on being addressed in Urdu; they said that there was no justice in the country, that the licence tax was worked in the most oppressive manner, and the Europeans were not *sahibs* in any sense of the word, but were far more akin to the European loafer to be found in India.

My American friend seems to be much amused at the idle carelessness of the colonials. Yesterday he tackled a lot of carpenters and masons, whose opening remarks suggested carefulness, but a supply of cigarettes soon made all square. The spokesman, a young unmarried man, gave him to understand that morality was not a leading virtue, neither was, apparently, industry, for he never got up till 8 and started work at from 9 to 9.30. An hour was taken for dinner at noon, and they stopped work at 4 p.m. The bosses were not strict—in fact, could not be—and the pay was good—18s. a day. Altogether he did not know where he could find a better country for an artisan. My American friend commented on the difference between Natal and the United States of America, where even the millionaires work from 9 a.m. to 6 p.m., and both master and workman toil strenuously all day, however much they may differ on the wages question.

A gentleman who was in the hotel with me, and who had, on his way out, visited India, inquired what I thought of Durban. My reply was that I was somewhat disappointed with the country, on which he let himself go and confessed that a short stay in Natal had turned him from an advanced Jingo into a complete Little Englander, if not a pronounced pro-Boer. He characterised the colonists as greedy, idle, unprogressive, and lethargic, who made money chiefly by subjecting coloured races to what was little better than slavery. My friend declared that indentured coolies were slaves, and that he did not think such colonies were of any use to England. He has been making inquiries as to trade, and has discovered that the rice trade is entirely in the hands of the Indians, the white merchants confessing that the Indians can sell rice at a price at which they cannot import it, do what they may.

I have again and again, with reference to the very common remark that "there will be no more Dutch wars, but a war with the Kaffirs is surely coming," asked, "Why is such a war coming? what is the reason for it?" and I invariably receive the same reply—"Oh, well, I do not know, but it is certainly coming; every one says so. There is the labour difficulty." There seems in reality to be no difficulty about labour; the men are there, and will certainly work if they are properly paid and get the fair results of their labour. The colonists will prevent any increase of wages if they possibly can, and also do all they can to stop Zulus or Indians rising above the position of beasts of burden.

A very hot day, and I have again been to the market; after all, I think, the stall-owners are white men, with Indian and Kaffir attendants, as only a white man could get a licence. All white men seem to smoke at their work and are usually not very civil. A tradesman from whom I bought a cap had been two years out, and admitted good profit, but was rather suffering from plague on the brain. He was not at all desirous of returning to England, but would like to go there on a visit.

I visited the botanical gardens a second time. They do not appear to me to be either nicely laid out or well kept. The trees are far too crowded for good effect; very few of them have name-plates, and where such exist they are frequently illegible. The place seems to have been arranged without any effort to secure landscape beauty. The annuals that do best in Bombay also do best in Durban, for frost is unknown here. Birds are few; small boys, using the filthiest language, fairly plentiful.

I am told that the Australian and New Zealand tramway men are not happy, and are contemplating getting up a corps to go to Somaliland. They say that they are not well received here, and that the prevalent distrust of one's neighbours makes life in Durban unpleasant.

A Russo-German, who had long lived in South Africa, mentioned to me as a remarkable fact that whilst in South Africa human beings are most cruel and brutal, yet animals are most tractable. He gave as an instance of a human tyrant a man of his own race. The same thing has struck me, and only to-day I witnessed two examples of bad temper and brutal treatment of horses. I ascertained the name of one very handsome shrub, rather like a creeper, that grows here. It is called *Alamanda volacea*, and is a native of South America.

An old Scotch gentleman, with whom I had a long chat at breakfast before leaving Durban, whose experience extended to before the days of railways, when Potchefstroom was the capital of the Transvaal, said that the Durban merchants were mainly forwarding agents; that Natal had grown rich out of the war; that the grant of self-government to Natal was opposed by the present Premier, who came out as a Royal Engineer officer and Colonial Engineer; and that he himself was disposed to think that it was a mistake, for each successive Ministry spent money on some fad or other and then went out. The Zulus in particular strongly object to the constant changes in the office of Minister for Native Affairs. The Under Secretary, it is true, is a permanent official, but they quite realise that, after all, he is a magnified clerk, so they do not look up to him. The Indians, he said, were under a permanent Protector of Immigrants who had been some twelve months in office, and was appointed by the Governor, with, he presumed, the consent of the Ministry; the Indians were thrifty, saving even out of their rice rations, of which they often sell a part. They were getting a good deal of land, and he did not like this, as they were dirty, untidy neighbours. It was, however, the fact that Natal would be a wilderness without them. The Kaffirs, or Zulus as they prefer to be called, are beginning to feel that they are a power in the land. They are not fond of work, but sometimes work well, and are physically powerful men. The Indians are far more industrious, regular, and reliable, with more intellect, but are not able to do hard navvy's work. At such work contractors now have to pay Zulus £3 a month, and cannot get sufficient of them at these wages; so much so, indeed, that a new railway from Maritzburg is stopped for want of men, and Zanzibaris at £2 a month and rations are being imported. Government, during the war and since, have been paying Zulus £4 a month. These wages my Scotch friend looked on as a grievance, but he quite admitted that all races had been rolling in coin to an enormous extent, and that there was some justice in letting the coloured races have a share of the spoil. As an example, white masons, and not hardworkers, had lately struck against a wage of 18s. a day. But he was not reconciled to the blacks having any rights, and looked forward to a native war. He said that Maritzburg was about as expensive a place to live in as Durban, and that though military officers received some extra allowances, they would find that it would take all their time to make both ends meet. It is apparently proposed to have a new camp at Maritzburg, with a garrison of 4,000 to 5,000 troops. The British people will, presumably, pay for these troops, and I really do not see the need of pumping money into Natal from income taxpayers at home and letting the Natal people govern as they please without paying any but the lightest of taxes. Bullying Indians and discouraging immigrants, even men from home and Australia, are parts of their programme.

CHAPTER V

Maritzburg—Military not popular with the civil population—Indian landholders—Buildings and roads—Town prosperous owing to the war—Sugar-planter's opinion of Indian coolies—Temperature and climate—Coloured labour indispensable—Mr. Chamberlain—Dutchman's views as to coming events—Police officer's account of the country.

On arrival at Maritzburg I found the thermometer in the hall standing at 90°, the air being, however, much drier than at Durban. The nights were cool and the mornings fresh. In regard to the journey, for the first two hours from Durban the train passed through pretty, well afforested hilly country, very like the immediate surroundings of Durban itself. There was a continuous succession of detached huts or European houses dotted along the line or on the hills around. Except for a little fruit which goes daily by special train to Johannesburg, the only cultivation was mealies, in patches here and there, often by Indians or Zulus, but at times apparently by white farmers. There were but few cattle to be seen, though the country seems to be well suited to grazing. The war has of course thinned out the animals. Small stores are to be seen occasionally, frequently run by an Indian. After two hours or so the country becomes tamer, and very like the downs at home, covered with rough, uncultivated grass, which appeared to be fairly green, but was becoming withered, as were the mealies, owing to want of rain, which has been scanty during this and the last two or three years. Numbers of Australian trees have been planted, and are now domesticated in Natal, amongst others the wattle, which is grown for the tannin obtained from it.

In front of our hotel some masons were employed in building new railway offices, an American passenger, who had spent his morning watching them, declaring that they took two hours to build what should have taken ten minutes, each mason having a Zulu in attendance, of course. My own view of the situation was much the same, as during the time I was at breakfast they sat with their legs dangling over the scaffold talking with each other—smoking, of course. Everybody smokes when at work here, even white keepers of market stalls when attending to customers.

A military officer, who had left India only five or six months, had noticed the ill-treatment of Indians and the feeling against outsiders which I have mentioned as prevalent in Natal. The colonials, he says, have a pronounced "chi-chi accent" like a Madrasi half-caste, and otherwise he thinks they are not dissimilar. The men in the shops and railways are, he says, never civil, and much given to using profane language, even when ladies are present.

In Maritzburg the only locally manufactured articles seem to be rickshaws and carriages; in Durban it was much the same, except that there was a saddle and harness factory. My Scotch friend of yesterday said that land had certainly enormously increased in value since the war, but that it had been steadily rising during the last twenty years, and had never once gone back. The newspapers refer to the prices now being obtained for land in Capetown. I remarked on this rise in regard to Johannesburg, and was told in reply that it was of course doubtful if it would last, but that it was quite likely that it would. The Rand mines would last for the next forty years, and in spite of all that had been written about opening up South Africa, the Rand magnates, who had millions invested, would take precious good care that there would be no opening up elsewhere which would compete with their interests.

At lunch I met a cavalry officer who had been six years

in South Africa, and was then stationed at the Mooi River. The climate, he said, was excellent, but dysentery was common and bad, and liver diseases prevalent. The military live a life quite apart from the colonists, who do not seem to like them, and rather resent, or at least are taken aback, if called on. They have lived alone so long that they do not want company. The Boers make themselves much more pleasant to the military, to whom they seem to have taken a moderate liking. A few of the sons of the colonists in the neighbourhood of the Mooi River (farmers) play polo, and play well. Society, in the English sense of the word, is non-existent, but that, to my mind, would make up for much else if the people were only truthful, just, and honest; but they do not seem to bear this character. My cavalry friend said that the military had, from the first, done everything they could to make themselves pleasant to their civilian neighbours, but to no purpose, as they certainly were not liked, and had in consequence to live apart from them.

The races were on, and my cavalry friend had in fact come to Maritzburg to see them. After some cogitation, and seeing the likelihood of a thunderstorm, I walked off to the camp, as cantonments are here called, instead. On my way down the well-kept streets of this quasi-quiet little country town, with more than half the houses one-storied, after the bungalow model, I passed several gay little gardens filled with verbenas, phlox, tiger-lilies, plumbago, and balsams, all of which were flourishing, especially the verbenas. The Natal Brewery has a very large well-built brewery close to the railway station, and, I am told, make good beer. Near by is a tavern, where no doubt the beer is dispensed, and further on the Governor's house, a large red brick building in a good-sized enclosure, high up and overlooking the town. I passed many shops owned by Indians where bread, soda water, vegetables, and other things were sold. The Indians are said to hold proportionately more land in Maritzburg than they do in Durban, and it is now proposed, I am told, to make them ineligible to hold land anywhere in the colony. The camp is up a hill beyond the railway station and gaol. The soldiers' huts are wretched structures, often built of corrugated iron, with small verandahs in bad order, very different to a cantonment in India. They are crowded together at the top of the highest part of the town, and have no signs of care or comfort. No doubt they are paid for by the British taxpayer. The garrison church is a plain but decent brick structure, built only a few years ago. It was turned into a hospital for four hundred men during the late war. There is a monument to the memory of the men of the 2nd Queen's who fell in the late war, giving nineteen as killed in action, twenty-one dying from wounds, and one hundred and fifty of disease.

The Maritzburg College, a nice-looking building, could be seen in the valley below. The storm, which I had anticipated, came on when I was within two hundred yards of the hotel. I found shelter, which was well, as there was a blinding black dust-storm, followed by hail and rain and peals of thunder. My Indian servant told me that he had never seen the like in India. The water ran like a river along the side drains, but in less than ten minutes it was over ; a bright, hot sun came out and a brilliant rainbow lit up the heavy clouds in front of me. The town is on the whole a nice one, and, I think, better built than Durban, a good description of red brick being largely used, also some stone. The new Town Hall and Parliament House are really fine buildings. Few houses have more than two stories, and fully half have a ground floor only. There appear to be no end of doctors, hotels, and boarding-houses. Some hides and tanning bark from the Australian wattle are exported, and there are several waggon, carriage, and rickshaw makers. The waggons are made very heavy, as in England, and not on the American pattern.

I found a military officer at Maritzburg in search of regimental stores which had been warehoused during the war with some military storekeeper, but he could find no trace of them, and was unable to fix the responsibility for them on any one.

This place is certainly hotter than Durban was during

the last fortnight. It should be, and usually is, cooler, being 2,000 ft. above sea-level. Yesterday the thermometer did not get above 85°, as against 90° on the day I arrived. The main roads in Maritzburg are broad, well metalled and well kept, and the shops substantially built and apparently large and good.

For the first time in South Africa I to-day heard Indians well spoken of by a colonist, evidently a man who had been a long time in Natal. Some one remarked on the jaunty air of a few Zulu youths who passed by the hotel on this Sunday morning, with the usual captious sneer as to the "air these natives give themselves nowadays." "Well," said the old colonist, "why should they not do so? They earn three shillings a day now, and why should they not fancy themselves a bit? Look at those two buildings going up across the road; more than half the work in constructing them has been done by Kaffirs or Indians. They made the bricks, and in fact have done all the work except the laying of the bricks." I remarked that only the preceding day I had seen a Zulu trowel out the mortar for a mason. The old man replied that but for the Indians there would have been no roads, for they made them all. Our captious critic admitted that natives worked well sometimes. "They always work well," retorted the old man, "and they are very good fellows."

The old gentleman told me that coffee was at one time grown rather largely in Natal, but the Kaffirs used to clear off and the crops were at times wholly lost, so that either the cultivation of this crop must have been abandoned or labour that could be relied on obtained. Hence the advent of the Indians, who have made Natal what it is. Now the Scotch colonists—for every one seems to be Scotch who is not an Australian or a Canadian—want to repress and practically enslave these men, because, to a small extent, they come into competition with them as artisans, merchants, and shopkeepers. A Scotchman holding these views acknowledged that the war had not only enriched the town people, but the farmers, who had sold their animals at four times the usual price. "You never hear a farmer complain now," he said. Incidentally he mentioned that local taxation was on value and not rental, and that it really came to about 4 per cent. on the rent.

The day following the races was very hot, 95° in the shade, whilst the next day it was 70° only. The climate varies very much, and dysentery is said to be very common. An old colonial I met on the hottest day gasped out to me, "This, sir, is a black man's country, in spite of all they say; it can never be made anything else." It turned out that he had sugar estates on the coast, on which he employed a thousand Madrasis, which no doubt accounted for his sentiments, as well as for his feeling the dry heat so much. He evidently did not sympathise with the current notion that Natal should be kept back permanently, for the farce of pretending that it is "a white man's country." Like all men used to any particular set of circumstances, he had not, as a sugar-grower on the coast, realised the extent to which the country is crippled by the restrictions imposed on black labour. He seemed to think that artisans would be welcomed, which is by no means the case. A tailor whose shop I visited told me that he dare not employ coloured labour, and that he has to pay £2 to the refuse of Europe for the mere making up of a suit of clothes. He says that he will give up making altogether, and sell nothing but ready-made clothes. He was in India once, and could easily, as he did in India, get all the clothes he could sell made by Indians.

Two gentlemen, Englishmen, travelling through South Africa, gave me a very unpleasant account of Johannesburg. One week of it was all they could stand. The town, they say, is filthy and the hotels bad. They are evidently much disappointed with South Africa, as all who have seen Johannesburg and the people seem to be. They wonder why we went so mad about the latter's grievances.

By the way, my sugar-planting friend says that he is certain that there are not more than 60,000 whites in Natal. There may have been 70,000 during the war, but many have since left.

Maritzburg has many pretty views over the surrounding hills, the slopes of which were at this season beautifully green; they appear to be cultivated, but in reality they are not. Flies and dust are a nuisance, and the place is smelly. The sudden changes of temperature must make the place unhealthy. The thermometer which registered 100° yesterday is down to 70° to-day, and the one which registered 95° is 73°.

The colony is peopled as much, if not more, by Indians as by white men, and the coloured people are an absolute necessity to the whites, but are nevertheless ignorantly and unjustly treated by the latter. The Governor of Natal should certainly be an Anglo-Indian official, whilst *instead of a Protector of Immigrants appointed by the Colonial Government and concerned with indentured coolies only, there should be a kind of Consul appointed by the Government of India, to whom all Indians, except the few who have votes, could appeal, because one-third of the Indians are non-indentured and their number is increasing.*

From what I hear and read it is evident that Mr. Chamberlain is becoming gradually aware of the present state of the Dutch-British question, and the character of those whose cause he championed. He is making up to the Transvaal Boers, and without promising anything, is "holding out hopes," which can be realised or repudiated as future necessities may suggest. He has also realised that, now that the Boers are temporarily scotched, his main danger lies with the Cape Dutch. Hence he is trying to pacify the Boers for the time being, and they will no doubt obtain all they can from him in his present conciliatory mood. It is to be hoped that they will obtain a written promise on the language question. In the meantime Mr. Robinson and other Rand magnates are falling away from the fold. There are, I may add, some who say that the present want of labour at the mines has been engineered, so that the war taxes imposed on the Colony may be minimised. Any way, since the sum was fixed, notices have been issued all over the recruiting districts that the reduction in the rates of wages which were paid before the war will not be enforced. To-day's papers publish a report that Lord Milner needs repose, as his health is not now good. Perhaps he is to be removed, to spare the feelings of the Boers.

My Dutch friend prophesied that as the probable result of Mr. Chamberlain's visit we are on the eve of :—

1. Hero worship of the Boers.

2. A mendacious crusade against the Cape Dutch. The newspapers are all under the control of the mining magnates, with special correspondents duly posted as to the line they are to take.

3. An equally untrue attack on the Kaffirs, in which the dangers to which the white population is exposed from them will be dilated on, and an attempt made to get up a Kaffir war.

4. A campaign in favour of forced labour, supported by specious arguments tending to prove that it is good for the Kaffirs themselves that they should be compelled to work, and that their wages should be settled by authority rather than by the only fair way of supply and demand.

The weather at Maritzburg has changed from hot to cold, 60° in the shade. These sudden changes do not seem to be good for work—at least, I do not find them to be so, as they seem to sap my energy entirely.

Strolling along Commercial Road, where there are a number of Borah shops, I had a talk with a decent Mohammedan, who complained much as to the hardships Indians experienced. A deputation had waited on Mr. Chamberlain, but had not been able to obtain any satisfactory assurances that their grievances, so far as they were on inquiry found to be real, would be redressed. He had received notice to quit his shop, which he rented from a white man, and would not be granted, he feared, a licence for a shop elsewhere, merely on account of his race. The people, who thus oppress the Indians, are always complaining of the boycotting habits of the Cape Dutch, contrasting their behaviour with the absolute freedom from discrimination that they are so fond of alleging prevails under British rule. Now the Indian shopkeeper in Natal seems to supply the wants of his own people and of the Kaffirs; consequently if he is eliminated the coloured races will be thrown into the clutches of a very low class of white shopkeepers, and the cost of living to them will be increased. Labour will no doubt be dearer in consequence, and all will suffer. The problem of South Africa is admitted to be a cheap and plentiful supply of labour, and this end will not be attained so long as the coloured races are not allowed fair play. Natal depends entirely on coloured labour, and it is therefore in the power of the Indian Government to secure their subjects from suppression. If the emigration of Indians was stopped for one year Natal would repent, and in five years repent in sackcloth and ashes.

The hotel at Maritzburg is fairly good. It is clean, the servants being either Madrasis or Kaffirs under white supervision, and no doubt the white superiors look on themselves as the workers. Both this hotel and the hotel at Durban have prospered exceedingly owing to the war.

Before leaving Natal I may say, what has several times been pointed out to me, that the Natal colonist, born in the colony, has an accent not unlike that prevalent amongst the country-borns in India, and to this is usually added a very sallow complexion.

It took seven hours from Maritzburg to Ladysmith. The country is hilly, with few trees, and those mostly gum-trees, which seem to do even better in Natal than Australia. On the banks of watercourses there are willows. Here and there a few Zulu huts were observable, with patches of mealies and some large farms, but mealies seem to be the only crop. The country was green with long, coarse grass, but, owing to the drought, not so green as it should be. In the cold weather it is said to be absolutely brown, and even now there are scarcely any cattle to feed on it. We passed one small cantonment with corrugated iron huts, and Tommy Atkins playing cricket. Near all such places there are Indian shop shanties of sorts. They creep up everywhere, and the Indians, as I have before observed, seem to be the most industrial and enterprising people in the colony in which they are so badly treated. On our journey we passed Estcourt, the lowest point reached by the Boers during the war. At this place there was a good railway station, and refreshments at the most moderate prices I have yet experienced—sixpence for a cup of tea and a large piece of cake, whilst the day before I paid one shilling for a bottle of ginger-beer.

In the train I met a young Irishman who had been in the police in Central Africa, but who had recently obtained a commission in the South African Constabulary. He expected to have to go home at once on sick leave, and gave it as his opinion that it was not conceivable that Central Africa could ever be of any use to England. He does not think that it can even pay its way, and it is thinly peopled and the home of jungle fever. The people he met were negroes, and not to be compared with Zulus. He seems to know a good deal of South Africa, of which he is very fond, the climate being so excellent on the high veldt. Durban, he says, has an enormous lot of crime, and is now full of white loafers, who have no intention of working, but who find their way into the police-cells. Many of them are even fashionably dressed. The young men arrive in the colony with some money, and ostensibly are looking for work, which they have no intention of doing. The artisans, who get eighteen shillings a day, are, he says, mostly a low type of Scot, and are by no means moral characters. Several prominent citizens were concerned in gun-running during the Zulu war, and during the late war one hotel-keeper was imprisoned for a year for selling Government champagne; another was fined for selling tools, the property of Government.

There is a good deal of patronage in the colony, which is frequently bestowed on near connections of Ministers, very few of whom, according to report, went to the front during the late war. My police friend says that the Dutch element is much the strongest in South Africa, and that eventually it will certainly control the country, but he repeated the common remark that a native war was near at hand. He could, like the rest, give no reason for such a catastrophe, except that the Zulus were getting independent, objected to the hut tax, and wanted more land to cultivate. It is a fact, he added, that they are at present very short of land. The reputation of several, more or less distinguished, soldiers, seems to have suffered in South Africa, and, according to my informant, they were found employment in which they could not do much harm.

CHAPTER VI

Ladysmith—Waggon Hill and Cæsar's Camp—Town prosperous—Railway journey to Johannesburg—Building contractor's account of the labour difficulty and rates of wages—Heidelburg railway station—Arrival at Johannesburg.

WE passed the Colenso river at night, but I could see that it was a narrow stream between banks, well wooded and perhaps 20 ft. high. Ladysmith is in a hollow and surrounded by hills, some quite close, and it does not appear to have been a good place to concentrate on. It is now very hot, and there is a perfect plague of flies. It is only a big village of the usual colonial type, the gardens being at present gay with bushes of plumbago, oleander, hybiscus, and pride of India, with a few flowers in which sunflowers are prominent. My servant tells me that there are two or three European shops only, but several kept by Indians. They were very useful during the siege, as they furnished large quantities of stores. Most of the house servants are Indians. They get as much as £4 a month and their food. I was told here that they are disliked because they can live "on the smell of an oiled rag, work hard, and are getting hold of property."

I started at 9.30 in the morning with a Zulu "boy" as Jehu, and two very lean horses, to see Waggon Hill and Cæsar's Camp. I drove up the hill, and then walked along it, in a very hot sun with the usual South African high wind, very dry and rather trying. The Zulu boy was in Cæsar's Camp with one horse during the war, and he showed me a flesh wound on his leg caused by a shell splinter. The boy tried to explain to me the various incidents which occurred during the attack. All the ground about the place is a mass of stones and boulders, and the Boers must have had great pluck to attempt the assault up a very rough and steep hillside. There is now a rough road up the hill, and a lot of sangars over it. I am told that the latter were all constructed "after" the attack. There are many mimosa bushes amongst the dried-up but grassy wilderness of stones, now covered with swarms of white butterflies. I saw several birds of sorts, including a lark; a snake which had recently been killed; and many pretty wild flowers. There are three little walled-in grave-yards, two in Cæsar's Camp and one on Waggon Hill. The monuments showed that most of the deaths were due to disease. The two main streets—good wide roads—seem to point to that part of Waggon Hill where the Devons made their charge. You seem to look right down on to Lady-smith from this commanding hill.

I had some difficulty in getting a room, and only succeeded in doing so through the kindness of a gentleman who insisted on my taking the quarters he had secured for himself.

There seems to be no reason for the fourteen to eighteen oxen still used to drag waggons here, even on good roads for short distances, and the reason is probably only an old habit formed when there were no roads and when it was as easy to trek with all one's oxen as to leave them at home. The waggons are themselves very heavy, and not at all after the light American pattern. The high wind is irritating, and there are heavy thunder clouds, frequently not followed by rain. The climate would not suit me.

On leaving Ladysmith, I may say that the hotel was run entirely by the Indian servants; the owner and his family occupying the best rooms and appearing to have very little to do with its management. They must be making money fast, as the charges are very high. I paid £2 5s. for four hours of the "Spider" and the two miserable horses, which seemed still to carry in their bony bodies the effects of the siege.

Before leaving, I asked an old stager what had been the effect of the war on Ladysmith, as one would naturally suppose that it must have suffered badly. He replied that of course it had suffered in deaths during the siege, but that it had much more than made up for any material losses, instancing the fortune which had been made by our host, the hotel keeper, who had converted a shanty into a large hotel. The water supply is not good, and there is much smallpox and typhoid in the town. The last Durban newspapers say that the natives are flying from the plague, and advocate the cessation of the issue of third-class tickets on the railways.

In the train for Johannesburg I found myself with one man only, a mason, travelling first class with a free pass. Three years ago he had not "the price of a drink," but now he had contracts in hand amounting to £25,000. The workmen, he told me, are absolutely the masters here, and that he had lost £600 in Johannesburg before migrating to Ladysmith. Masons, he says, cannot be got in Johannesburg under 25s. a day, and then they only lay 600 bricks daily against 1,000 at home. In India a native mason lays 600 for 8d. to 1s. a day. My friend is not at all averse to employing coloured labour. He mentioned that he had great difficulty in getting materials; he had twice had to stop work as he could not obtain 20,000 bricks. Masons, he says, are very cunning in spinning out work when they do not see bricks ahead of them. "They are not going to work themselves out of a job, you know." He is now, in Ladysmith, paying masons 18s. a day, the regular rate being 2s. an hour, as against 9d. or 10d. at home. His best job, he said, had been supplying "boys" (Zulu Kaffirs) to Government at 32s. 6d. a month, whereas he paid the men only 20s. himself, and moreover kept ten days' pay in hand, which means a good deal more, since large numbers of them leave their ten days' pay and go home. He had been foolish enough, he said, to take a partner, who took frequent holidays, however much the business suffered. A few colonials, he said, worked well, but the majority were lazy and useless, whilst the colonial women would do nothing, and if they made a small purchase in the market must have a Kaffir to carry the parcel home. How are such people to develop the country? Only a complete change of policy will ever do it. What Natal wants is the encouragement of coloured races who will work instead of their being oppressed in an underhand way. There appears to be no doubt that Mr. Chamberlain, one of whose complaints against Kruger was his treatment of our Indian fellow-subjects, has openly said out here that they should be kept out of the Transvaal, and their numbers in Natal largely diminished.

The train journey to Johannesburg was comfortable enough. We had coffee at Standerton and breakfast at Heidelburg (the site of the Coronation Reef), which is rather a pretty-looking town, with plenty of planted trees and some decent looking stone and brick buildings, including a conspicuous Dutch church with a steeple. The country seen during the daylight is all veldt without a tree, never-ending grass, at present green, but brown in winter. Here and there were the remains of burnt farms, with people now living near them in miserable make-shifts of the everlasting corrugated iron type. Most of the domesticated animals have disappeared, but there are a few pigs, goats, horses, and cattle near the villages, such as they are. The Kaffirs look miserable, in old cast-off European clothes. It is a pity they have no distinctive dress of their own. One farm I saw all spic and span, which my solitary companion, a Dutch storekeeper, said belonged to one of those who disgraced themselves by becoming national scouts. "They sold their country, for without them the English would never have taken it." There are, he said, some 15,000 of these men, with whom the rest of the Boers decline to have any dealings. I was surprised at the number he gave, and think that the figure must be an exaggeration, though I have since heard the statement repeated.

All along the line are blockhouses or the remains of them, barbed-wire fences, and small graveyards, with heaps of old empty tins and camp refuse. Nothing could look more deplorable, and I could not help recollecting, having just read in a history of South Africa that the Zulus were never once known in all their wars to have molested women and children. My Dutch friend got in at Greylingstad, a little station with three or four houses, mainly corrugated iron, one of which was grandly named in large letters "The Scotch Stores," and another "The Grand Hotel." It turned out that my friend and a Scotchman kept the former, and the stores mostly came from Holland. He was a thoughtful, sad-looking man, as all Boers or Hollanders whom I have met are. I remarked on the well-built Heidelburg railway station; "Built by the Dutch before the war," was his proud rejoinder. It was far better than most of such buildings out here, so that I respected his feelings. The air was very nice coming along this morning, and we found Johannesburg, for once, without wind or dust.

CHAPTER VII

Johannesburg—Feeling of despondency and insecurity—Transport difficulty—Sir W. Butler and Lord Milner—Indians in the Transvaal—Climate—White and black labour—Looting during the war—Mr. Chamberlain and the labour question—Kaffir wives—Price of land in Johannesburg—A clergyman's opinion as to the state of the town, also on the manner in which the war was brought about—Increase of prices since the war—Including the Boers, the majority of the white population of Johannesburg came from South-Eastern Europe—The English birds of passage—The coming Kaffir war.

As told to me, things in Johannesburg are not very satisfactory. Those who have known the place for years do not look hopefully on the immediate future. Large numbers of people have come from Europe and elsewhere with a little money in hand, which they have been liberally spending in the hope of good times, now that the war has ceased. But shares, with one or two exceptions, have sagged, in spite of Mr. Chamberlain's visit, and the newspaper reports of Boers dragging his chariot refer, it is said, to the National Scouts, of whom I have lately spoken. It is also said that the labour difficulty is mainly due to the reduction of wages, and that this, again, may have been partly resorted to with the view, as the mine magnates thought, of obtaining better terms from Mr. Chamberlain, if the mines were not too prosperous when he visited them. Anyway, there is a great feeling of insecurity as to the future. The banks are said to be very cautious in advancing money, and it is asked what will happen when those who have made money during the war, as well as those who have come out with some cash in hand, have got through their assets and are still without work. The new Government is very unpopular as any Government must be amongst such a heterogeneous and ill-disciplined crowd. They would be satisfied under no Government, but at present their cry is said to be, "Oh, give us back our old Government and Kruger." After all Kruger did not press his laws home, and the self-same laws (characterised as brutal before the war) are now being administered to the letter. The Indians say that nothing has been altered in their favour, whilst the white men complain that what Kruger's Government did for them in ten minutes now takes two or three visits, of several hours each, to get carried through. I know nothing as to the truth of the matters on which these views are based, but merely repeat what seems to be on everybody's tongue.

This day's local newspapers advocate the dismissal of the nominated Municipal Commissioners and others being elected by the citizens, foreigners not being allowed to vote. Before the war all Britishers were foreigners, and one of their chief complaints was that they were not allowed to vote, the very practice complained of being now advocated by them when in power. Well may Mr. Chamberlain say that the war was due to a misunderstanding. Men, I may add, appear to be chary of giving their opinion to strangers, as spies are said to abound. This, I fancy, is not the case, but it points to a feeling of suspicion and distrust being abroad. It is admitted that the police have been greatly improved under the new *régime*, and a number of our good friends, the London Metropolitan Police are seen similarly dressed in the streets. In innumerable other respects, the Government, my informant says, has gone back, but he has nothing but high praise for the new police. The railway, he says, is trying to get back some of the old Dutch hands.

The next morning I took a stroll after breakfast and had a look at some of the chief streets and the market-place, where the very dirtiest and most evil-looking lot of loafers that I ever saw were collected. Sales of corn, mules, &c., were going on in Dutch and English. A cow and calf went for £23, which, according to the auctioneer, was "giving them away." There are certainly some nice streets and shops, and the advertised prices of common kinds of clothing did not seem to me to be particularly high. At the hotel, Lager beer is 4s. a bottle. My servant has moved to a boarding-house, kept by a Mohammedan, where he gets a room to himself and decent food for 3s. 6d. a day—at the hotel he was in a tiny room with two others. The Madrasi boys, who wait at table, get £8 a month, and their food, but their washing costs £1 10s. a month, as blacks are apparently not allowed to wash for the public. The charge for washing a collar is consequently 6d.

There seems to be great difficulty in getting stores from the coast. An official says that, though given special facilities, it often takes him two months to get up cases from Capetown, and one of to-day's papers says that the robberies *en route* are enormous, sometimes whole consignments disappearing; at other times the contents only being pilfered. In neither case does the railway give compensation. This enormous transport difficulty is rubbed into me everywhere.

The South African Constabulary is very much in evidence here, and at the railway stations I noticed that cycles were very numerous, whilst in Natal they are scarcely used at all. In speaking to a senior kind of official in the hotel office as to postage, he inquired if I was a new arrival. When I told him that I had come from India, he said, "That is the country that all the 'Tommies' like so much. They are delighted when they hear that they are to go there." I suggested that Standerton, where was a camp that he knew, did not seem to be a lively place, and that soldiers probably found much more fun in India. He admitted that it could not fairly be so described, but it was his place. He also told of a wound in his leg, and how he was with one of seven columns all out after Botha, whom they did not manage to catch, though they made up for that, he said, by entirely destroying his house, a beautiful place in which there were two pianos, worth £300, which were burnt, and for which, no doubt, the English income taxpayers will have to pay, though the recollection of the incident evidently gave my friend infinite satisfaction. He was inclined to disbelieve the rate of income tax which I told him was levied in England, and when convinced on that point evinced a disinclination to continue the conversation.

I am glad to find that some inkling of the true state of the labour case has reached home, though Mr. Chamberlain has said that to speak of men, working under contracts, as slaves is nonsense. As a matter of fact such contracts can be, and are, made much more like slavery than free labour. Moreover, no one who studies the question on the spot can for a moment doubt that the nearest possible approach to slavery is what the white colonial and mine-owner are driving at.

I was glad to see a Reuter telegram in which Mr. Ritchie is said to have remarked that every soldier in South Africa costs £50 a head more than in England, exclusive of the cost of building barracks, which must be enormous with the mason-cum-carpenter rule prevailing. The British taxpayer will, under these circumstances, be inclined to object to more wars, or to a large military force being kept in South Africa.

I had a chat with a Manchester business man last night. He is merely travelling round. His opinion of the commercial morality of the place is a very low one. Ordinary honesty, he declared, is laughed at, tricky agreements of all sorts and kinds being the ordinary and daily practice.

Most, if not all, of the Indian officers who worked the railways during the war have left, and the British officers remaining are loud in their complaints as to the expensiveness of the place. Hotel rates are high—£1 a day being the lowest charge. The military force in Natal is, I hear, to be largely reduced, unless the colonists agree to pay for it. The same story as to a probable Kaffir war, for which England is to pay, is current here, the object of the projected war, so far as I can ascertain, being to cow the Kaffirs into working at the mines. The whites will not do hard physical work, so the Kaffirs must. That is the theory, and I have little doubt the mine-owners will carry it into practice if they can.

I am greatly amused to read in one of to-day's local papers that the people at home are very ignorant and very easily imposed on, if their newspapers are worked properly, and that it will be necessary now to prepare them for the action contemplated. A Cape colonial whom I met said that he thought the present composite Cape Government was quite right in the line they were taking "because there is no doubt that the Boers are the best people out there." But as they are here in the majority he does not believe that responsible government can be given in the new colonies for years, as the Boers would swamp the English, who on their part are clamouring against what they call Kindergarten Government. The name Kindergarten alludes to Lord Milner's young Oxford subordinates.

I was told here by an officer who had served under General Butler that the General was right, and that the war was quite unnecessary; in fact, he seems to me to be a regular pro-Boer, and it appears as if I shall soon have to look in vain for a military officer who does not belong to that disreputable body. He also speaks of the wholesale looting and burning of furniture that took place, one volunteer concerned in the furniture trade being very active in that respect, observing that such destruction was "sure to lead to a boom in the trade later on," a prediction which has been fulfilled. It is sad to listen to these stories, even if they are only one quarter true, and no doubt there is much exaggeration; but there can be no doubt, I think, that Great Britain's reputation suffered considerably in the hands of local volunteers during the war. It is said here that Sir W. Butler resigned his South African command rather than send up troops to Mafeking, a step intended to force Kruger into declaring war. Lord Milner is said to be a clever, bookish, weak man, who was completely under the thumb of Cecil Rhodes, and that the latter for one reason at least desired war—because he was quite unable to influence Kruger. This statement agrees with what was told me two-and-a-half years ago by a gentleman who worked for years under Rhodes, and who stated that the latter's theory was that all men could be bribed, and that whilst, no doubt, he usually succeeded in South Africa, yet he failed entirely with Kruger. The war was a good business, I am told, for contractors for supplies, some of whom sent in cards when submitting tenders bearing addresses in the most fashionable parts of London.

I explored the slums where Jews, Chinamen, and Indians jostle each other. They have many corner shops, and a policeman told me that they were doing well. I had a talk with a man from Surat, who was here for three years before the war and then went home with Rs. 1,500. He has now returned and amassed another Rs. 1,000 with which he proposes to return to India at once. I warned him to avoid Durban, on account of the plague scare. He, however, is of opinion that Natal is better for Indians than the Transvaal, where he thinks there are only 500 to 600 of them. They nearly monopolise the fruit trade, but find it very hard to get licences except by bribery. However, they do manage to get licences sometimes, partly through four Indians who have some way or other got on to the Municipal Council of Johannesburg—been appointed, I suppose, by Government. Wages, he said, were very high, so were expenses, and the work demanded was hard. The climate of Natal was, in his opinion, better than that of the Transvaal. Clouds of dust made the evening a perfect pandemonium. How people can endure such a life is wonderful to me. Lung diseases are common. In the winter the dust is worse, I am told, and the cold is also great at this elevation of over 5,000 ft. There are very few fireplaces. The mornings are by far the best times in South Africa. So far as my experience goes wind and dust are constant after 2 p.m., yesterday one could only shut oneself in the house, and there the flies were troublesome; they are, however, bigger and better behaved than the little wretches which abound in Maritzburg and Ladysmith.

I strolled in one of the suburbs and crossed the river near the Wolhuter gold-mine, up to the ridge overlooking the town. Jocoba Street is here being laid out, and a few small houses are being built. I never saw such jerry building anywhere. One four-roomed house was being put up, walls mostly one brick thick laid in mud, no scantlings on floor or roof thicker than two inches. The latter was of sheet iron nailed on boards of common pine. For this single-storied house, which was to have a separate kitchen and bath-room, £22 10s. a month was to be charged. Two-thirds of the small houses in this suburb are of corrugated iron throughout. The corner shops in the poorer parts of the town are kept by Indians, with, I think a few Chinese—at least, I saw one of the latter. The Indians seem, however, to be chiefly hotel waiters receiving £8 a month and their food, or to be fruit and vegetable hawkers. So far apparently Indians are allowed to pursue these avocations, and to this extent, to participate in the great profits made in the colony, which the colonials avowedly endeavour to keep for themselves. Australian gum-trees have been largely planted, and have rescued Johannesburg from its primeval bleakness and bareness. These trees and a few others are to be found thickly planted in the better part of the suburbs, and are a great relief from the sun at this season. The roads are still often not macadamised, and are very dusty.

Kaffirs are said to get £3 a month, with 3 lbs. of meal daily, and meat and salt once a week. The gentleman who gave me this information, an ultra-colonial, said that if England interfered in the colour or labour question all the whites, Dutch and others, would join and "sweep the coloured people out of existence." He declares that the coloured people are well treated, and asks why England pays its skilled sailor labour less than he pays his Kaffirs. I demurred to the correctness of the statement, and inquired why sailors, in that case, did not come here and take the place of the Kaffirs. Apparently he started life as a sailor himself, and so has a special sympathy for the handyman. It seems to me that though white men here avoid hard physical labour, they still do much more of it than they do in Natal.

People here speak of the wealth amassed by the Natal colonists during the war, and say that very few Natal colonists volunteered for service. Natal is said to have completely got round Mr. Chamberlain, because when the spontaneous offer of two millions is looked into it will be found that no money passes, but that certain charges due to the colony for coal used during the war were withdrawn, transactions on which the colony still made a profit, and never expected to fully recoup. This fact, it is believed, is now well known to Mr. Chamberlain.

The proposal to import Chinese is not popular, and I am told that the Boers would not unlikely join the workmen in resisting such a step, as they have had sufficient trouble with one coloured race. All colonists with local experience seem to think that to give the two new colonies self-government, at present, would land the British where they were before the war, namely, under the Dutch, who are admitted to be the better people, at any rate outside Cape Colony. In the meantime the townspeople are agitating for an elected council, some present thinking this to be a good move, whilst others are not in favour of it. I am inclined to think that if elected Municipal Councillors are allowed, elected Provincial Councillors will soon follow.

The feeling against coloured people is very strong. One mine-manager with whom I talked, said he would like to exterminate the Kaffirs and work his mine with white people only. I am told that he is somewhat of an enthusiast, and that his views are not shared by his employers. My other friend—the one who loves the sailor—is greatly concerned that people should come here from home and get such wrong ideas concerning the treatment of coloured people in South Africa. According to him, they are too well off, and too well treated, whilst there is no ill-feeling against them. Which story am I to believe? At dinner all present were very hot as to the Transvaal being a white man's country.

The next morning I saw some railway works, in which large gangs of Zulus were employed, with only one or two white foremen to supervise. When we came to carpentry, all were whites on seventeen shillings a day, but each carpenter had a Kaffir to attend to his wants. I asked the railway official who showed me over the works, and who was present at the dinner of the previous evening, "Where is your white man's country? I see none of it, beyond the fact that no man of colour is not only not encouraged, but not allowed to rise beyond the degree of the unskilled labourer." Later on I was shown some few white men unloading trucks, doing for ten shillings a day precisely the same work for which the Kaffirs working alongside of them were paid two shillings. I was told that the whites were employed on the work partly to avoid their being thrown on the hands of the public for subsistence.

My Manchester friend was very angry because a colonial from Natal remarked in a loud tone that "If England loses her colonies it will be because of her folly in interfering in the labour question." The cool effrontery of this suggestion, after the sacrifices made by the Mother Country, was too much for him. Another Natal colonial said that Lord Milner was getting impossible, as he was completely in the hands of the mining magnates, three or four of whom ruled the whole of South Africa. He was, this Natal man declared, as much disliked by the colonials as by the Boers, and the idea of his underlings is to prevent free government as long as possible, since when this came about they would lose their appointments. The Transvaal authorities are apparently not very sympathetic where Natal is concerned, that colony, it is freely stated both by officials and non-officials, having given very little assistance during the war. It is said that very few Natalians entered the Transvaal, those who did so being generally refugees, who had been driven down to Durban when the war broke out. In all, fourteen Natal colonists are said to have lost their lives in the war. There are all manner of stories of wholesale loot during the war and of inconsiderate acts, like the removal of the brass name-plates of distinguished Boers at Bloemfontein, which have greatly enraged the Boers.

I accosted an oldish man, who looked like a workman of the better class. He came, he said, from Yorkshire, to which county he retired during the war, leaving his wife and children in Johannesburg. For thirty years he had been touring with a circus in India, China, South Africa, and chiefly Australia. He said that the war had entailed great losses on both sides, "Yes," I replied, "and the worst of it is, that somehow I never feel certain that it was necessary." "It never was necessary," he answered. "I lived here, you may say, before the town came into existence, and I never had anything whatever to complain of against the Boer Government; in fact, I did better before the war than I do now, because so many Jews have come in and cut prices till one can hardly make a living at my trade, which is that of a house decorator."

The newspapers are getting hotter and hotter on the labour question. What they really desire is forced labour, procured by paying the Kaffir chiefs to send down their young men, whether they are willing or unwilling to come. This is thought to be a better plan of hoodwinking the British public than direct crimping. Mr. Chamberlain, when asked what help Government could give, said that in this respect they must work out their own salvation. This reply, it is argued, leaves them free to take such steps as seem best to them. Mr. Chamberlain also told a number of Kaffir chiefs that he had been authorised by the King to say that they would be protected in every way. The King, as a matter of fact, has no power to protect the native races against the white colonist in a self-governing colony, as the Indians in Natal have several times been plainly told by Mr. Chamberlain himself, and before long the Transvaal will be in that position. The newspapers are following up Mr. Chamberlain's rather ignorant lead, that the only slavery in South Africa is that of the Kaffir wives, who grow the mealies whilst the husband idles. It does not seem that matters would be improved by the husbands being taken away to work in the mines, and the wives left to do both the field work and the house work, and to the latter they violently object.

The prices of land in Johannesburg are very high. One stand or plot, with a 50 ft. frontage and 100 ft. deep, lately sold for £32,000, and another is now for sale for £50,000, which sum, it is not unlikely, will be obtained. There seems to be a general feeling that the price of land will fall; but it is just possible that it will not do so in the main business centres of the town for some time at least. All salaries are paid monthly here, and most men at once put their savings into mines, hoping to become millionaires. In the hotel at which I am staying the chambermaids get £6 a month and their food, and the Madrasi waiters £8, with food also. In a brewery the fitters get 27s. 6d. a day, and the Kaffirs £3 to £4 a month, with quarters and food. Local beer is retailed at 6d. a glass. The brewery pays 15s. a thousand gallons for water.

I had a very pleasant interview with a clergyman, who says that there may now be 70,000 whites in Johannesburg, possibly more; there were never so many before the war. He says that there was great depression for five or six years before that broke out, and he does not understand what the people are living on. He evidently thinks that bad times are ahead, though later, things may mend. Rents, he says, are now often taken in advance, and every one, he thinks, is keen enough to go to the cheapest market without regard to the nationality of the seller. Certain nationalities are said to absorb certain trades; thus plumbers and bootmakers are nearly all Russian Jews, whilst bar-keepers are mainly Germans. Wholesale groceries are chiefly in German hands, and the clothing trades in English. Ready-made clothes, which are mostly worn, are nearly as cheap as in England. Preserved milk is sold at a price which can leave little profit.

The clergyman's opinion is that the war was a terrible blunder, and personally he declined to believe that it could take place until the very last moment. Before the war the English language and literature were slowly but surely making ground in South Africa, but that is less so now, and, instead of the two races blending, they are terribly apart. The war was, in his opinion, brought on by those who thought they could make money out of it, and they made haste to bring matters to a climax, whilst the existing English Ministry was in power. The money expended on the war would, he thinks, have more profitably been thrown into the sea, and will have no effect in anglicising South Africa. The Transvaal will surely follow in the wake of Cape Colony, which is mainly Dutch.

There can be no doubt as to the eventual result, as the Boers increase in numbers much more rapidly than Europeans who settle in South Africa. Amongst the Europeans, the preponderance of men, and of young men, who do not intend to permanently live in South Africa, is very noticeable. Their idea is to make money and leave. White people will, the clergyman says, only work in South Africa for one generation. Those born out here will not work, and so large a proportion of them become wrecks that he sends his sons to Europe to be educated, though his wife is a colonial born. Very few whites, he says, really work in South Africa, but those who do so always get on, and they have a much better chance than in Europe. The great majority live on speculation, and in the end most of these fail. Drink, speculation, and ill-health, the first and last being frequently caused by the worries of speculation, account for nearly every failure he has met. It seems to be a riddle to my friend how the present population lives. Nor does he understand what is behind the thirty millions the Transvaal mine magnates have promised towards the cost of the war, but he believes that they had some scheme connected with it in reference to labour.

The cemeteries at Johannesburg are better kept than those at Durban. Trees grow remarkably fast out here, and flowers, when cared for, also do admirably. Only water and care are required to grow anything. Even in the cemeteries all the work is done by Kaffirs. I only saw one white man, a mason, and he had two Kaffirs to help him. One grave was covered with lovely petunias and lobelias. The trees were of the usual funereal description. The police, dressed just like, and partly taken from, the London police, seem mostly to amuse themselves with examining Kaffirs' passes. Butchers' shops abound, even in the suburbs; they are always dirty, whilst the meat looks anything but appetising. The summer is said to be hot, but I do not think that it is nearly as oppressive as August often is at home. I am told by a long resident that, though the climate is not hot, Europeans lose their energy in South Africa, even up in the Transvaal. After three months' residence one begins to feel tired and sleepy, and this feeling increases on most people. He says—though I have not noticed it—that there are many Dutch in the town, and that they are keen men of business, and often great rascals.

I called on an English lady, an old acquaintance, whose husband has long been in business in Johannesburg. She says that the cost of living in Johannesburg has increased immensely since the war. Many things—washing, for instance—have doubled in price. Houses which here now let for £100 a month would not fetch more than £80 a year in an English country town. The post-office and railway management are worse than ever, and altogether the only good that has come out of the war is, she considers, the English flag. It seemed to me to be clear that she would be only too glad to leave the place at once, and, in any case, she means to do so next year, to take her children home to be educated.

An English gentleman in my hotel propounded the theory that the English have nearly reached the stage at which the French arrived long ago, and do not really want colonies, as they no longer go out to colonise, except to make money and to return home to spend it. We have not really got colonists, he said, though we still manage colonies for other people. In support of this statement he added that in Johannesburg not more than 30 per cent. of the white population, the Boers being excluded, are British, the remainder mostly coming from the south-east of Europe; and I must confess that my experience on shipboard, and what I heard of other such vessels, lead me to the same conclusion. The Yorkshire house decorator said the same thing. Such British as do come to Johannesburg mostly leave their wives and families, if they have any, at home, because a married workman, so my informant assures me, cannot live on less than £20 to £25 a month, even if he has a small family. That is to say, a respectable carpenter, with a wife and two or three children, must have from £250 to £300 a year to live on in decent comfort.

My friend does not believe in the expected phenomenal growth of Johannesburg. He says that, before the war, there were never more than 10,000 white men employed in the mines, and 100,000 Kaffirs; and that, as there is no other industry but mining, the rest of the population must be parasites on those employed in the mines. The whites never get less than £20 a month, compared with £4 for a Kaffir, so that any very great increase in these numbers is improbable. Altogether, my friend has come to the conclusion that, however England may keep the colonies going, it will be almost entirely for the benefit of Jews, Greeks, Poles, and Russians from the south-east of Europe, also, of course, for the Boers, whose smallest family is said to be ten. As an example of prices, I am told that mutton is 2s. 6d. a pound, and that a turkey costs £3. Medical fees are said to be three guineas a visit, but a doctor told me that not more than one-third of their bills are realised.

The only decent church in Johannesburg belongs to the Roman Catholics; the Church of England parish church is not a creditable structure for so wealthy a community. There is a very good local white stone, but there is also a buff-coloured stone to be had near at hand which I think mixes better with red brick than does the white stone. It is used in the lower story of the Mutual Buildings in Harrison Street, plaster being substituted above. It looks well, especially when slightly roughed. I found an open place, used as a market, monopolised by Indians, who were selling ready-made clothes, combs, brushes, Jew's harps, and so on, to Kaffirs. Many were Suratis, and the rest Bombay Mohammedans.

Dining with a German, who is a pro-English Jingo, but whose wife has Boer sympathies, I heard much about the Boers. There are, my host told me, far greater contrasts among them than amongst the people of most nations. Some of the Boers are the nicest men imaginable, others quite the reverse. They used to treat the Kaffirs very badly, but have not done so for many years, because if they did so, the men would leave them for the mines and other employment. He believes that sufficiently good pay and reasonable treatment will attract all the labour required, and he also thinks that mining magnates, for some reason or other, have been keeping labour away rather than trying to get hands of late. No native, he says, is by law allowed to hold any land—a law as cruel as it is impolitic. He says that no attempt is made by Government or the whites to improve, or in any way to educate, the natives, who, on the other hand, are, he says, very quick and apt to learn. They are great talkers, and can argue in a wonderful way, being most clever diplomats. The English do not understand them nearly as well as the Boers, having had less experience of them. They blow hot and cold, one day spoiling and the next day ill-treating them. The present cry of slavery of the wives is entirely ridiculous; the men attend to the cattle, shoot, and do many kinds of work, but the field cultivation is done by the women, who have not got the smallest objection to the custom, or any idea that it is an unfair division of labour. It is odd that people with such good mental powers have never invented any system of writing.

The next day I passed the market square, where any number of auctions were going on, largely of cast-off army horses. The South African weariness, of which I have spoken above, appears to be affecting me, as I feel very tired and useless to-day. It is said that the white men cannot stand prolonged hard work here, and that by their own exertions they can never make agriculture pay. If this is true there can never be a really healthy future for the country, as there certainly will not be for Natal, until the coloured races have a free field to carve out their own fortunes. Neither will the Transvaal be cheaper to live in.

A New Zealander I have been talking to here, who had, owing to his experience of the Maoris, never fallen in with the general feeling as to the coloured races, told me that he thought that these were certainly unfairly treated here. He is the second New Zealander I have met, and both hold the same views, though both have been long in South Africa. The other whites appear, on the other hand, to have very much adopted the Dutch ideas, which have descended from the days of slavery. They would re-establish the "institution" throughout South Africa to-morrow if they could. This is really at the bottom of all the labour suggestions of the colonists. My present New Zealand friend has been eleven years in Johannesburg, and thinks, as I do, that the future points much more to gloom and decadence than to Lord Milner's dreams of mutual wealth and glory. He thinks that the Dutch will quietly abide their time, that they will steadily prepare the ground, and when the mines work out, if not sooner, will be the real rulers of the country. According to popular theories of government, this is exactly what they should be, as they are not only in a majority, but in a large majority. The British are afraid of responsible government, though a noisy minority of mining magnates are in favour of it, as they hope thereby to establish forced labour, which they would do with the concurrence of all the whites, Dutch and British. They fear that whilst under home government their *bête noir*, Exeter Hall, will prevent the establishment of anything of the kind. They, of course, do not really care a pin who governs, provided that the mines return large profits, as not one of them will remain in South Africa once the mines are closed down. The new colonies and Natal will, in my opinion, then almost cease to be white colonies at all —at any rate so far as the British are concerned.

As I write an often-repeated knocking has happened at a room door. It had become annoying, but at last the door is opened, and I hear a remark addressed to one of the independent white porters, who occasionally make the hall lively with their oaths. "Oh, I thought it was only a coloured 'Boy.'" These little side lights show what the feeling is towards all coloured people in this country. Such an atmosphere must deprave all but the strongest characters, which accounts for my being told that the British who come here are usually, at first, shocked at the treatment of the coloured races, but rapidly get worse than the people who have been here from their youth. A young Englishman, who says that he can talk seven native dialects, and who is firmly impressed with imperialism and the beauty of slaying one's neighbours, informed me that he is anxiously looking forward to the coming Kaffir war "which will settle the native question," the meaning of which phrase is difficult to understand, unless it means forced labour; in no other respect can natives be worse treated than they now are. He has not much respect for the Natalians, who, he says, will never make a colony; but as regards the other colonies he is of the new school, who think that Great Britain should be tied to the tail of the Colonial cart, because he says that the Canadians and Australians make better soldiers than the British, though he admits that the South African colonist makes a worse one. He is a fine-looking fellow, and anxious to be allowed to solve the labour problem and make his own fortune. Neither the responsible authorities nor the mining magnates, however, seem to fall in with his views. On my putting it to him that no one would care to work down in the bowels of the earth unless well paid for adopting the disagreeable avocation, he said, "Yes, the question of wages is at the root of the labour difficulty." He says that he himself can do anything with the native races because he is most punctilious in treating them fairly, and scrupulously keeping his word, an elementary virtue which, he says, is rarely, respected out here, even by Government. He is very down on the Cape burghers for being so rebellious, but he says that their attitude in this respect is due to repeated acts of bad faith on the part of Government. He declares that quite a million sterling is due to the Kaffirs for supplies they brought in during the war, and he relates to me a story of how he himself procured some supplies. Our talk ended by his telling me that thirty shillings a day has been demanded of him for the hire of a cart and harness without any horse, so that the loyal colonist must be doing fairly well just now.

The Jews here, as elsewhere, seem to be large landowners, many valuable plots of ground being pointed out to me as belonging to them. I found several Eurasians doing fairly well in Johannesburg, and from what I learnt about their families it seems to me that in emigration to Natal might be found a solution of the Eurasian difficulty in India. Kaffir "boys" do all the hard work which is so distasteful to the Eurasian wherever he may be found.

I have bumped up against several men of various degrees whom I knew in India and who have moved on to South Africa to "better their position," but the result seems in every case to have led to disappointment, since they find few of the comforts and none of the luxuries of India, whilst the pay to be earned is very little more, and purchases very much less.

CHAPTER VIII

Journey from Johannesburg to Pretoria—Arrival at Pretoria—Kruger's house and church—Bad effects of the war—Pretoria clean, well laid out, and apparently prosperous—Indian shopkeepers especially useful to the Boers—Some of the Indians prosperous, others barely make a living—Views of an Englishman who had been twelve years in the country.

THE railway to Pretoria passes for some miles through continuous gold-mines, otherwise being undulating and bare except where a few gums, willows, or other trees have been planted. After a time the mines cease, and grassy downs, broken rarely by a Kaffir farm, are only observable. As Pretoria is approached—the distance between the two towns is only forty miles—the ground gets more hilly, and the soil more barren, until the valley, in which the town is situated, is reached. The latter is commanded by forts on the neighbouring hills, and the train passes through a narrow defile before reaching it. The streets near the railway station are ill-kept and dilapidated, and until the market square is reached, the shops are not very inviting. At that place there are several fine-looking Government buildings in stone, and several fine shops. The hotel where I stayed is owned by a Hollander, and is kept beautifully clean. Our host retired early, as he told me that it was his turn to be up by 4 a.m. At a glance it could be seen that the hotel was managed, and it is the only one in South Africa, I have so far found of which this could be said. The servants are mostly Hollanders, civil and friendly, who seem to take a pleasure in making the guests comfortable. The hostelry is made up of several little detached cottages, a system common in Indian hill stations and well adapted to this warm, sunny climate.

It was sad yesterday to pass through miles of long grass, for hay is, I believe, never made in this country; and we also, I think, saw as many graves as heads of living cattle. The place reminds me of an Indian hill station in June. The waiter complains of the heat, which he feels very much. It is, however, in his opinion, infinitely preferable to Johannesburg. I entirely agree with him, and would much prefer to live in Pretoria to any place in South Africa that I have yet seen. It is quiet, and, I think, cleaner than any place I have as yet come across. It is difficult to understand how so many shops can be supported, but Pretoria is a great distributing centre for the Boer farms. I saw some waggons being loaded up with flour, groceries, furniture, and other things, evidently for use in the outlying places. The Boers are said to never fail in paying eventually, though they take their time, and at present must necessarily have long credit.

There is, I am told, very keen competition in all trades, which seems on the face of it to be likely, since in this small town or big village there are, I should say, more and bigger shops than in an English town with three times its population. There is only one distributing centre north of the place, viz., Petersburg, so there must be a large country trade.

There are many Indians here, Borahs and Suratis, and they have some quite decent shops even in the neighbourhood of the principal streets. They are also cleaner and better dressed than I have seen anywhere else in South Africa, and I am glad to say, usually stick to their national dress. The daily paper has an article urging Government to stop their hawking licences, for many here seem, as in Johannesburg, to be hawkers.

Flies are very troublesome. Grapes grow splendidly in the open; some vines in the hotel garden have large bunches of hothouse-looking grapes on them. The market square has the Palace de Justice and the Government offices (the old Parliament House) on opposite sides, and in the centre a large Dutch church. Close by are the base and pedestal of the Kruger statue that was about to be erected when the war broke out, and on which I have no doubt in time his monument will rest. After all that can be said, Kruger will in time to come, I am satisfied, be recognised as the Transvaal Grand Old Man. The President's house is a very unpretending building, practically a one-storied cottage, having marble lions on each side of the doorway which were presented to Mr. Kruger by Mr. Barney Barnato. Opposite the house is a fine street, on the opposite side of which, and approached by a neat footpath, is a church built for the ancient President by his admiring friends. It is surrounded by a large out-spanning enclosure, now beautifully green. The usual stories of vandalism, that really become monotonous and depressing, are rife. The marble lions seem to have escaped because they were too heavy to take away.

There were a great number of bicycles in the streets; in fact, they have been in evidence everywhere since we left Durban. From the labels in the wine-sellers' shops the usual price of whiskey seems to be six shillings a bottle.

The Artillery Barracks, which cost £250,000, are a handsome group of buildings, and a credit to the Boer Government. Mr. Kruger built them out of the indemnity he received from the Jameson raiders. Local military officers seem to prefer the Boers to the Uitlanders, for whom so much has been done; and speak very strongly as to the absence of any commercial morality in the place. The whole country, in their opinion, has suffered from the demoralising taint that war always leaves behind it, to which the speculative character of the mining industry has added its bad effects. Not even did the army itself wholly escape, it seems, from evil tendencies.

The Indians, I notice, walk at present on the pavements, whatever they may have done previously, and generally appear to be more comfortable and more prosperous in this, the only really Dutch town I have seen, than elsewhere.

There are lots of evident Boers about, all in mourning, and I constantly hear the Taal dialect spoken. The Indian shopkeepers are useful to them in supplying the wants of their Kaffirs much cheaper than the white shopkeeper can, and as farmers they should have no desire to expel the Asiatic retailers. Labour is said to be very dear here, Kaffirs getting £3 a month, and the prices in the shops have not gone down since the war. The population of Pretoria is at present believed to be about 23,000, including 7,000 soldiers.

We drove one day to the Zoological Gardens in an American "spider," drawn by two good mules. They occupy a nice site and are well laid out, but they are untidy and not well kept. The Cape leopard cat is a very pretty animal. There is no doubt that this little town, now the headquarters of the Transvaal Colony, as formerly it was of the Boer Government, is the nicest one I have so far come across, Maritzburg coming second, but this place is more homely, and the people generally look cleaner.

The Indians seem to be better off than elsewhere, and adhere to their national dress. Stopping a hawker to buy matches (price 3d. for four boxes), we found that the man, a Borah, had come from Porebunder, on the Kattiwar coast. He was here for two years, but left before the war began. He was then in India for three years, and had only been back for two months. He denied having had any trouble here in the days of the Boer Government or at present. Even the Kaffirs are better dressed, and look to be more prosperous than elsewhere. The roads are wide and well laid out, but few of them are paved or properly metalled.

It is a wonder that the Boers did not bleed the Rand more and spend it on the capital. Had the place been a Crown colony for the last fifteen years, there would certainly have been an expensive Government House, and roads like billiard-tables for the officials to drive along. These luxuries will have to be reckoned with in the future, unless a free government is established, but that is a contingency which, in the interests of the coloured races, I trust will never occur. The Boers also seem to be against it, as their three representatives refused to join Lord Milner's Council.

The Indians in the Transvaal, many of whom are now being given seven days to clear out, as they came in without passes, have only themselves to blame if they find the change of rule is bad for them, since they foolishly joined in the appeal to Great Britain against Boer oppression. It is quite likely, on the other hand, that their grievances were manufactured for them by the other Uitlanders, and that they had little really to do with the matter. Anyway, it seems to me that the Boers, who never keep shops and only come most reluctantly to a town when forced by necessity to buy or sell, were much more likely to encourage Indian shopkeepers, who sell cheap to their Kaffir farm hands, than a Government either composed of or dictated to by white shopkeepers and artisans, who abhor the very name of an Indian or of a coolie, as even the high officials ignorantly call all natives of India.

As I have before remarked, the British military officers do not seem to have a good opinion of the colonials. One officer remarked to me that it was a lucky thing that their character was not known before the war broke out. It is, however, open to question whether "unlucky" would not be a more fitting adjective. Those officers who have served in India are very angry at the treatment which Indians receive in these colonies, and say that they cannot believe that the Colonial Secretary is aware of it, or comprehends that they are British subjects, who have as much right to live in the Transvaal as any Englishman. They are, however, being turned out daily, and it is clear that unless the Government makes a stand, they will shortly be worse treated than ever. Mr. Chamberlain has, it seems, been talked into the position that there are too many Indians in the colonies—the indentured Indians excepted—since the latter live solely to enrich their European masters.

On leaving Pretoria I have nothing but good to say of the hotel, except that the prices were high, especially 10s. a night for my servant's bed on the floor. All prices are high. Ordinary bricks cost £5 10s. a thousand.

On Sunday, during our stay in Pretoria, we visited the Indian quarter to the west of Pretoria, which we found much larger than we expected. There were large numbers of Kaffirs there, all much better dressed than we had seen elsewhere. Their houses are built of corrugated iron, as is the case with those of nearly all the poorer whites and many of the well-to-do. Amongst others we met a very smartly dressed Indian, riding on one of the few clean bicycles I have seen in South Africa. On accosting this individual it turned out that he was a *dhobie* (washerman) from Agra, who had been twelve years in the Transvaal, though he did not appear to be more than thirty years of age. He had now a large laundry, and employed thirty assistants. He had saved £3,000, and meant to return to India shortly. The Indians had not, he considered, ever had any proper grievances in the Transvaal. The difference between India and the Transvaal was, he said, that in the former country thieves usually got clear away, whilst here the detectives were too many for them. The number of Indians in the Transvaal had largely diminished since the war. My servant says that there are two classes of Indians in the Transvaal—one class makes money, whilst the other has not in hand the price of a meal.

In the train between Pretoria and Johannesburg I talked with an Englishman who had been twelve years in South Africa. His views were as follows:—

1. The Dutch are all liars; you cannot believe a word they say.

I suggested that possibly the Dutch did not consider the English colonials particularly trustworthy, and he admitted that he himself was of that opinion.

2. That, do what Government could, the country would never be at peace, but that South Africa would always be like Ireland, the difficulties here not being nearly over.

3. That unless something could be done to cheapen the cost of living, so as to bring Britishers into the country, the

Transvaal would soon become a second Cape Colony, by which he meant that it would become practically Dutch. Prices for necessaries are still as high as during the war, and much higher than they were before it. British workmen, except skilled artisans, could not live in the Transvaal, and are better off in England. The idea of British farmers starting with £300 to £400 was, he said, simply ridiculous, and would court failure. The Boers, who wanted nothing but a few white clothes, could no doubt live, but not Britishers.

4. That there are many more British shopkeepers in Pretoria than before the war, though they always predominated. The number of Indians has diminished.

5. That notwithstanding the number of English shopkeepers, they manage to keep up prices, and are making money fast.

6. That he thought the price of land in Durban and Johannesburg would go down, but not at present, as just now there is more speculation in land than in mines.

7. That the ideal in the colonies was to make large profits out of very little labour. All would rather grow short crops than sell cheaply, and no one took any trouble about anything. This explains why frozen meat, which is carried all over South Africa in refrigerating cars, is so much used. Eggs are never less than 1s. 6d. a dozen, and enormous quantities are imported from Madeira, whilst bananas can be bought cheaper in London than in Durban. People will not be bothered with such "trash" as eggs, and even despise rearing cattle. A friend of his had lately cut down his walnut-trees because it was too much trouble to pick the nuts, for which he could only get 8d. a pound.

CHAPTER IX

Return to Johannesburg—Permit regulations fail to exclude undesirables, whilst they cause much inconvenience—Journey from Johannesburg to Capetown—A railway manager on black labour—His surprise on learning that, in India, coloured people are not subject to restrictive regulations—Repudiation of Cape Colony public debt under discussion previous to gold discoveries in South Africa—Boers predominate in Pretoria and thence to Capetown prevail.

On my return to Johannesburg I went to a new hotel, which was no improvement on the old one. On going out I met a Surati pedlar, who was here for three years before the war and has lately returned. He had no complaint to make as to treatment either before the war or at present. Trade was very bad now, because the mines were not in full work. He preferred India, but it was easier to make a living here though expenses were very high, £2 to £3 a month being paid for a very small room. The Europeans out here were none of them men of any account, and were quite different to the sahibs who lived in India.

The landlord of my hotel, a German, says that in spite of all the fuss about permits, the undesirables have got back, whilst honest people have been put to much inconvenience. Three months ago he went to Durban and engaged a German cook and maid, but after fruitless trouble to get passes for them he had to leave them behind. His view is that, at present, there are no satisfied people in the Transvaal except the Boers, who are getting help to rebuild and restock their farms. Every one else is full of grievances. In explanation he said that, except the Boers, all the rest had come to make money and go away. They did not wish to work, and many would not do so under any circumstances. "I have to make the best of it and employ them as they come, but as soon as they get £10 together they move on." The town is not now making money, so every one is angry and dissatisfied. They say, "We do not want the franchise—it is of no use to us; we want money."

Johannesburg is full of idle, thieving rascals, and robberies are common. It is difficult to see how a country is to be built up from such a population, none of whom wish to stay there; whilst those who are forced to do so are disgusted and dissatisfied. My landlord has been for eight years in the place, and evidently is making money fast, as all the hotels are now crammed, and have been since the war. Servants are, he says, the chief difficulty, as they not only demand tremendous wages, but are also impudent and unpleasant to deal with. He added, "They will not let Indians in, as they wish to keep the business in their own hands." Every white servant wants at least a couple of Kaffirs to look after him, and meetings are now being held with the object of forcing Government to exclude Indians. The hotel improved on acquaintance, and the bill, for Johannesburg, was moderate.

My ticket to Capetown cost me nearly £20, and we had as a railway companion an English military officer, stationed at Johannesburg, and for part of the time the manager of one of the railways, who is a most enthusiastic admirer of South Africa, and a great believer in its future. He considers it is a white man's country, and objects to coloured men being employed except on the roughest kinds of work. He looks forward to the time when white men will do every kind of manual labour, as in Australia, but he admits that white and coloured men will never permanently work side by side. He could not explain how the white man is to monopolise the work so long as the cheaper coloured man is at hand. At present, he said, sufficient Kaffirs are not to be had, so that whites and Kaffirs work together, the former getting treble or more pay for the same amount of work. The excessive cost of living in South Africa is, he admits, mainly due to the restrictions placed on coloured labour. The railway manager was much surprised to hear that Indians in India were, in respect to employment, subjected to no restriction of any kind, and that as a fact some of them held very high positions in the Government service with corresponding emoluments, and that otherwise they got their full share of profits in commerce. In a tone which left no doubt as to the sincerity of the avowal, he expressed a pious hope that such a state of things would never exist in South Africa, and he certainly would do all he could to prevent it. He stated, however, that Kaffirs can hold land in Cape Colony, and that they do so ; he was not aware that they were under any disability in this respect in the Transvaal. Of course the old laws can be modified, unless they have been stereotyped by the convention made with the Boers. He was much in favour of responsible government being given to the new colonies at the earliest possible moment, and was strong in his opinion that South Africa was the freest land on earth—a freedom, I mildly remarked, which did not appear to extend to coloured men of even older civilisation than our own ; an Indian, for example, not being allowed to be out after 9 p.m., and not being allowed to buy liquor, though they are notoriously a less drunken and a far more docile race than Europeans.

My railway friend told me one remarkable fact, viz., that some fifteen or sixteen years ago, when Cape Colony was hard pressed, the idea of repudiating the public debt was uppermost in the minds of some of even the leading men, and that but for the discovery of gold it would, he feared, have been adopted. He mentioned the fact, not in connection with existing political circumstances, but as showing the present wealthy state of the country, and its credit, when money can be had for 3 per cent. He thought that it supported his views as to the future greatness of South Africa. It is a fact which may well be remembered by the British investor, not in regard to South Africa only, but other British colonies which are at present not too prosperous.

The railway from Johannesburg to Capetown may for all practical purposes be taken to pass through entirely uncultivated veldt of the most dreary description, getting more barren as the Karoo district is reached. Odd farms are to be seen at very long intervals, and these usually consist of some cattle-grazing and a few mealies. Over all this long distance there is neither in the European nor the Indian sense cultivation at all—rolling veldt of uncultivated grass, with, in the season, even little that is really green, and hardly a tree to be seen. Here and there, where water is near the surface, there are a few acacia bushes. Often the veldt is stony, but there must be a great deal of land which would respond to the labour which one looks for in vain.

The Boers are the only people who work outside the towns, and they must do far more work than the British colonists allow. Their strong, shuffling, ungainly walk, their spare, muscular build, their horny hands and stooping bodies, all point unmistakeably to constant labour or outdoor exercise of some kind. The railway manager remarked that when he first began to give piecework to white men in unloading waggons, Boers came forward and did fully 30 per cent. more than Britishers could compass, no doubt because they were used to hard work in this climate. Although the Transvaal and Orange River Colony is Boer country, I had seen very few Boers in or around Johannesburg that I could recognise as such, but Pretoria was evidently Boer except for the shopkeepers, who are always foreign, and mostly English. Once away from Johannesburg, and all is changed. Dutch was the language most talked in the train, which, I believe, carried General de Wet, though we did not see him. One could not help admiring those fine, grave-demeanoured men, often of great size, the very double of the best class of North British farmers. My military companion I found to be most enthusiastic in praise of them. He declared that, in spite of all that I might hear to the contrary, they showed magnificent bravery during the war. He himself saw them charge, knee to knee, right up to the muzzles of the deadly Maxims.

After entering the Karoo country the veldt ceases to grow grass, its place being taken by apparently leafless and dried-up scrub, about twelve to eighteen inches high, relieved by greenish bushes of ice-plant, or something of the kind, which is said to be very good food for sheep and goats, Karoo mutton being the best in South Africa. We saw a few flocks of sheep, but hardly any cattle at all, except in a succession of trains laden up with sheep, goats, and oxen, all being imported from Australia, Madagascar, and elsewhere. The goods trains are being loaded up with these and building materials, to make good, at the expense of Government, the ravages caused by the war. As you get into the Karoo country the gently rolling veldt becomes more hilly, and even mountainous, until at last it becomes a rugged, inhospitable mass of rocks and crags, the bare rocks very much split up by the lightning, which is such a feature in South Africa. My military friend had a brother officer struck dead by his side a few months ago at a committee meeting in a tent.

We were still in the midst of this desolate scenery, making one imagine that the Almighty had cursed it for some great sin, when night came on (our third in the train), and on waking we were not far from Capetown, the country being now more peopled with a considerable number of cultivated patches and many houses and farms, evidently mostly Dutch, and looking by no means uncomfortable, with nice gardens, vines and vegetables. Even, however, right in Capetown there is no regular continuous cultivation such as is common in Europe or India. The soil seemed to get more sandy as we approached Capetown, but no doubt with care and water it will grow anything. There are, as Capetown is approached, lots of flowering trees now growing wild, but originally planted; also many gums and other Australian trees, often planted by the Dutch for the sake of shade.

CHAPTER X

Capetown—Hotel—Further remarks on incidents during railway journey from Johannesburg to Capetown—Dutch and English inhabitants of Capetown apparently irreconcilable—Cape Colony very prosperous as the result of expenditure incurred on the war—Cheap labour indispensable but lower class whites opposed to immigration—Agriculture very backward—Dutch must, by force of numbers, eventually rule—Indians, Malays, and other coloured races better treated in Capetown than elsewhere in South Africa—Fruit excellent—English Church not flourishing—Simonstown—Dutch the prevailing language in Capetown, and spoken by the coloured races—Sir W. Butler—Wynberg—Cape Civil Service—Constantia—Farming prospects in South Africa—Mr. Chamberlain's visit—Dutchman on the situation in Cape Colony and the Transvaal—Municipal matters.

CAPETOWN is very striking at first sight, and will, I think, be a pleasant place for a fortnight's stay. The hotel is quite beyond anything I have so far seen in South Africa, and up to a good London standard; the charges being, I fancy, about the same. Robberies from guests' rooms are, however, said not to be infrequent. The baths and sanitary arrangements are excellent and the tables are clean, nicely laid, with decent linen and cutlery. The food is sufficiently good and fairly well cooked, the bread and butter perhaps not quite up to the mark, whilst elsewhere they were often the only redeeming features of the fare.

As a postscript to my account of the journey from Johannesburg to Pretoria, I may add that all along the railway were the usual blockhouses, one was quite ornamental, whilst others were very substantially built of cut stone. There was barbed wire everywhere, festooned for long distances with empty jam tins, so as to give long warning of the approach of the Boers. The skeletons of dead horses and cattle sacrificed to the foolish mania of man, lonely little cemeteries, enclosed by more barbed wire, and an occasional burnt and pillaged farm, completes the picture of this long and gloomy journey of 1,014 miles; all the way I never saw a wild animal and rarely a bird. A fellow-traveller recollects when, in the same districts, great herds of various kinds of deer and other South African mammals were common. The white men in this country seem to have wiped out every other kind of creature, and, excepting the Boers, not to have much increased in numbers themselves.

My military companion during the journey was overjoyed at the thoughts of getting away, though he had for some years been in India, Somaliland, and so on, and might on return to duty be again sent to a locality of the kind. He was for some reason or other sent to a lonely place during the war, and his one admiration seems to be for the typical Boer farmer, whom he describes as very like the farmer of his own country (Scotland)—sturdy, independent, civil, and even kind, but very ignorant. The occupant of a farm, which he was required to visit during the war, asked, "Why do you want to take our country from us. What have we done to merit such treatment?" This my companion gave as an instance of the Boer's surpassing ignorance, though it seems to me that the Boer farmer was not so very wrong after all. Being, as my friend of course was, firmly convinced that annexation was for the Boers' good, he, by some process of reasoning, was enabled to regard it as an entirely different thing from the annexation of Alsace and Lorraine, though I must confess to a personal bias in favour of the Boer's contrary point of view. After one of his bursts of admiration, as numbers of these tough old warriors, curiously garbed and nearly always in mourning, got out of the train, he suddenly asked me, "What do you think of the future of the colonies?" I parried the question, and on a following day, when he returned to the subject, I pointed out that he had been three years in the country, and asked him why he had made the inquiry of a mere passer through, such as he knew me to be. His reply was, "Well, unpleasant as it is to think of or speak about, I do not think the prospects are good, nor do I believe in the peace that Mr. Chamberlain is now preaching, and I do not think that the two races will ever be reconciled. Moreover, in time the Dutch are bound to swamp us." His opinion of the loyal colonists for whom so much blood had been shed, and so many millions spent, was the reverse of high, and I left him counting the hours till his vessel should sail, and praying that he might never again set foot in South Africa, despite its splendid climate. "I wish," he said, "that we could forget all about the past and our dealings with the Boers, for there is simply nothing to be proud of in the whole thing from beginning to end." The one thing that impressed me on the journey, in which all my companions agreed, was that it was no white man's country: the glistening sun showed that very clearly.

After engaging my berth on a steamer leaving in the middle of March, I went by train, to visit a friend living in the suburb of Claremont. I found him occupying a very nice house facing the green but precipitous side of Table Mountain, and separated from the road by a paddock and quite a little forest of fir-trees. A beautiful weeping oak stood close to the verandah, and the large and lofty rooms were suited to the place. The climate did not seem to me to be as oppressive as August at home, though the sun was powerful. The nights are said to be cool, and the thermometer rarely reaches 80° in the verandah. In returning I made one or two small purchases, the prices charged seeming to me to be moderate. I was served by an Englishman, who told me that the usual wages of shop assistants were from £10 to £12 a month, and that it cost them, including tram-fare, £6 a month to live in the suburbs. I noticed that a Malay was helping, nominally as a cleaner, but the shop assistant said that he was quite competent to serve at the counter.

I met numbers of people of different positions, and they all seemed to be pleased with Mr. Chamberlain, but were all of opinion that the apparent peace would not last long. The Colonial Secretary has no doubt done as well as circumstances permitted, but the old sore, which brought about the war, remains, and is not a bit healed. The British here will never rest unless the Dutch adopt their views, British ascendency included, and as this is never likely to happen, the British colonists have a bad time before them. What they wished was that the Colonial Secretary would suspend the constitution, and hammer the Dutch into shape. This has not happened, and to my mind they will grow sulky, and that before long. For my part I trust that Great Britain will turn a deaf ear to their persistent and arrogant claims to an ascendency that they merit neither by numbers nor character. The sooner they understand that they have got to pull with the Dutch, or sink, the better for all parties, except perhaps the coloured population, who can only be helped by England; for no white man in South Africa will do so, if he can avoid it. There seems to be a feeling among the richer set of colonists, who have made such fortunes out of the war, that the Cape ought to contribute to its cost. There is a pretty quarrel on the subject, the Ministers, who are said to sympathise with the Dutch, declining to move in the matter, on the perfectly fair ground that one of the reasons given by their opponents for suspending the constitution was that they were sad squanderers of public money. A contribution to the cost of the war might, they say, be adduced as a further instance of unjustifiable expenditure. The Cape people are unquestionably most prosperous just now, as a result of the millions that the war has brought out here. Fifty million sterling at least have stuck in the colony, and not a penny has been added to the taxation. I hear recriminations on all sides, amusing in their way, whilst I carefully abstain from saying anything myself. Mr. Chamberlain's last lecture here is said to have been given wholly for home consumption. My friend, a high official, remarked that on every principle of political economy there ought now to be a slump in land values, but he doubted if such would take place, since he believed that the whole of South Africa was now immensely rich. The military, he remarked, had been pouring riches into the country, and the colonials have correspondingly benefited.

The cry everywhere is for more labour, yet the legislature has just passed a restrictive measure which the lower class whites pointed out to Mr. Chamberlain as not restrictive enough. It is complained that though the war is over no land is available for British settlers, and Government is urged to buy up land round the railway lines and re-sell. The Government, it appears, has very little public land, having granted what they had to white men, as the natives were killed off in successive wars. It also seems that two acres are usually required to keep a sheep, and in some parts eight acres, so that a farmer to do any good requires at least 6,000 acres. Agriculture is out of the question, as only irrigation, which means cheap labour, can render that possible. Just round Capetown, as at Constantia, is, so far as I can ascertain, almost the only real agriculture in South Africa, though I believe that in the Orange River Colony some may also be seen.

I asked a lady of Dutch descent, though for many years in England, the wife of a friend, if she found that her old Dutch friends and relatives had been changed by the war. The reply was yes, but that they now avoided all reference to politics, and in that way she got on all right, though the younger Dutch had ceased to call on them. She said that she could not understand all this difference, because twenty-five years ago Dutch, French, and English got on as one people, intermarried, and had no race difficulties. "It is most absurd," she added, "because they all talk English, and *are* English, but they now stand aside." Things do not seem to have improved compared with years ago.

Mr. Chamberlain has left, and to-day there are letters in the *Cape Times* which are not calculated to please the Dutch. Messages will reach England before Mr. Chamberlain does, which will not strengthen his faith in the possibility of wiping out by a few honied words not only the deaths of

20,000 women and children and the wreckage of a whole countryside, but the angry suspicions begotten of impotent fear. The words and the spirit that prompted them are no doubt genuine, but they have, I fear, come too late, and they are certainly not approved of by the British Colonists, who are bitterly disappointed that the Colonial Secretary did not denounce the Bond. The Dutch were not even given to understand that henceforth they must consider themselves a humbled and inferior race to the South African British colonist. Mr. Chamberlain's attitude seems to be that Great Britain has stepped in and wiped out the two Republics in order that South Africa may become one country, governing itself by an elected (white) legislature, the majority in which will rule, irrespective of race. But the British colonists know quite well that, unless they can disfranchise or in some way jerrymander the Dutch, power must pass, and in all probability quickly, into Dutch hands; the war having hastened the evil day by uniting the Cape Dutch and the Boers, who until the war were never friends, and often on the point of becoming fighting enemies. A good many of the more respectable and settled Britishers will join the Dutch party, I have no doubt, for it is the best party in South Africa. How, then, will the unstable and money-grubbing Jingo minority find comfort in the Colonial Secretary's counsels of perfection? It is a pity he did not make his tour in South Africa in 1898 instead of in 1902. In that case, if the same spirit had then animated him, England would not have spent three hundred millions to make the Dutch paramount in South Africa, as they are certain to become unless the British element comes to its senses, and accepts the Dutch as equals in every respect. If they do so they will be absorbed into the Dutch rather than the Dutch into the English. In any case the attempt to treat the Dutch as a conquered or inferior race is certain to fail.

In regard to commercial matters I am told that the tendency in Capetown is for the middleman or merchant to be eliminated, and that manufacturers' travellers now come out from home and take orders. In India a similar practice prevails. In Capetown I find that there is still some kind of a line drawn between the merchant and the shopkeeper, though, with two or three exceptions, merchants do some retail business in a quiet way.

On the following day I drove with friends to the Bishop's house, and then to Mr. Rhodes' place. We went through very pretty oak and fir woods, both kinds of trees doing splendidly here, though the former grows too fast to make good timber, for which purpose neither kind of tree seems to be made any use of. Both species were originally brought from Europe, and the Dutch are very fond of oak avenues, of which numbers exist. The fir avenues remind me of Japan. We passed some dozen Punjabis at work clearing timber roots, with a European in charge. They had only been here some two months, and did not seem to be happy. Fruit is cheap enough here, if bought wholesale, but very high prices are charged by retailers, there being few small shops. Malays are numerous, but do not seem to be much assisted by Government, as their sons are not allowed to be educated beyond a certain standard. Many of them are, however, well-to-do, so that they could without difficulty start their own schools, and in many cases they even have votes, so that they are in a position to fight their own battles. Practically it seems to me that Easterns are better off here than elsewhere in South Africa, one sign of which is that no objection is raised to their using footpaths or riding in tramcars. There is, in fact, a far greater admixture of all classes in Capetown than elsewhere, and mixed races of all colours abound.

All along for some two hours' drive the country was very pretty, and we passed numbers of nice houses with large gardens, orchards, and vineyards. Many of the old Dutch estates have been bought by speculators, and divided up and sold at a large profit, which almost invariably goes out of the colony. Within my friend's recollection many fine old houses and properties have passed from Dutch hands, the race appearing to be unable to hold its own with new-comers after the third or fourth generation. Certainly the surroundings of Capetown are very pretty, and the climate and fruits excellent. I was given a pear that could not be beaten, and splendid grapes are sold at threepence a pound—I fancy for a third of that price wholesale. Peaches and nectarines are very fine, and, I should say, are grown with very little trouble, much care about anything in South Africa being rare. The roads, too, are better here than in the newer towns, and the houses are very much better. Marseilles tiles are gradually replacing corrugated iron and slates, which in many cases have in these towns superseded the old Dutch thatch, but a good deal of this still lingers on. Rickshaws and bicycles are very little used. Johannesburg was phenomenal in its cycling population.

The cathedral at which I attended service on Sunday is a very miserable barn-like structure, and it is contemplated to build a new one, for which the army, if you please, is being requisitioned for subscriptions. We happened to be there on the occasion of a big volunteer parade service, so the church was full, otherwise I am told that it would have been nearly empty. Generally the English churches in South Africa are not flourishing. The Wesleyan Methodist and other churches are more cared for and better built, but religious feeling is not strong, except in Natal, where it is mixed up with business enterprise. Ladies are by no means regular in church-going, and children are often not taken to any place of worship, both of which advanced fashions do not fit in with the slow Dutch notions of the fitness of things.

One day we went to Simonstown, which is some thirty miles distant, the route lying at first through pretty suburbs, and then between Table Mountain and Table Bay, with rocks and sands on the seaward side and continuous mountain slopes landwards, which became rapidly more and more dotted with villas, boarding-houses, and so on, until Simonstown is reached. Here a large Government dock is being commenced, on which two or three millions are to be expended, and from which the colonists will draw a rich harvest. The flag-ship and several men-of-war were in the harbour, which is well protected, but not very spacious. The admiral has a nice house, and there is a naval club. A small street of shops and houses makes up the sum total of the place, which entirely lives for and on the navy and the British taxpayer. There is a capital service of trains, which on Sundays brings out many Capetown people to the various and increasing number of seaside resorts on the route. I was told that but few Dutch people lived in the houses round, that they always left, as the country became suburban, but that they held on to their land as long as possible.

A young colonial who joined us on the excursion did not seem to hold the orthodox opinions of his class, as he declared that Lord Milner was ruining the country, and that he had enraged the Boers by not fairly carrying out the treaty promises in regard to education and the disposal of the gift of three millions. He was insistent that Government should make no attempt to do away with the Dutch language, as such action would, he felt sure, tend to increase its use. It is odd, by the way, to notice how universally Dutch is spoken by the coloured people, who are a very mixed race, Indian, Malay, and St. Helena blood being mixed up with Dutch in such a manner as to render identification difficult. I suppose that half the population of Capetown is coloured, and all apparently speak Dutch, though some also know a little English. They can all own land and have votes, even Kaffirs. There is no curfew. The result is that the coloured population of Capetown are happier and more comfortable than elsewhere, and the whites show less contempt for their darker fellow countrymen than in other parts of South Africa.

My English friends are, however, far from satisfied with their prospects, and are doubtful if they will remain in the country, though pressed to do so by relatives. The lady says that she feels that there are troubles ahead in South Africa. She says that the root of all the troubles has been the determination of the English colonists to ride roughshod over the Dutch, and that so long as England can be relied on to back up that stupid and arrogant feeling, and in doing so to pour millions into the country, the English colonists will never cease to treat the Dutch as a conquered people. The colonists know perfectly well that whether considered as plucky fighting men or in regard to general behaviour the Dutch are well able to hold their own, and if Mr. J. Chamberlain's visit has the effect of making it clear that the Old Country is henceforward going to see perfectly fair play, possibly things may mend, and the English colonists cease to pose as superior beings. It is doubt, however, on this point that makes several of my friends, who have done well for themselves and their families, look forward with fear to the future. Many of them are ultra-British, but at the same time they recognise the facts as they are, and their recent experiences, coupled with twenty-five to thirty years' residence, have, it is evident to me, shaken their faith in the wisdom of the policy advocated by the colonial loyalists. The queer thing is that no one ever hears such views in England. I have tried again and again to get at the root of the South African difficulties from all sorts of men who have resided there—military officers, officials, and independent men—but they invariably kept their own counsel and appeared to know nothing. Here in Capetown it is very much the reverse; the home-bred officers without exception speak strongly of the many good qualities of the Dutch, and even the wealthier colonists, who do not directly say so, imply as much. With the least encouragement out it comes, as an awkward fact, especially after such a war, and for such a people. This opinion may be a consequence of the war, but the universal belief out here, save amongst a few colonials born and bred, is that if the Boers are by no means angels and have many bad habits, still they are by far the best human products of South Africa, and as such they must, in the long run, win, provided they do not deteriorate, and there is no apparent reason why they should. Rather the contrary, as they are likely to be better educated, as a whole, in the future.

There are many stories about General Butler, who moved a good deal amongst the Boers, whom he liked, and from whom he learnt more truth than from the exaggerated stories that were studiously circulated before the war. Hence he knew the real strength of the Boer position, and declined to move troops in directions which would, he said, have the inevitable effect of forcing the Boers to declare war. Thus the only man who was right in his reading of the writing on the wall was called a pro-Boer, and he was recalled in order that war might ensue. Doubtless the Colonial Secretary was not aware that his friends' estimate of the Boers' strength was so erroneous. An army chaplain, who has been out one-and-a-half years, and is about to return to England, told me that he was delighted to leave the country, which has, he says, nothing but a good climate to recommend it.

In strolling round I inspected the new Town Hall, and got into conversation with the head mason—an Englishman—who has only been out six months, and is now sending for his wife. Rent, he says, takes one-fourth of his wages. The stone-cutters under him are working on imported Bath stone, and get 13s. to 14s. a day, which sum, he says, is none too much, as the expenses out here are "cruel." He could not tell me what the stone cost when dressed ready for fixing, but he thought rather more than double what it would at home.

The next day I went to Wynberg, and was much struck by the very pretty roads and nice houses, buried in firs and oaks with juniper and plumbago hedges. I did not find my friends at home, and occupied myself with reading a letter on the labour and taxation question in the *Cape Times* which exactly fits in with the views I have formed since coming out here. It is signed "G. Ingham," but I have no idea where the writer hails from. I do not think that any up-country or Natal paper would have printed it, but down here in Capetown, where the coloured man is so much more intermixed with the white workman and often has white blood in his veins, besides always knowing a little Dutch, there is not such a contemptuous, and I may say brutal, feeling of antipathy to colour, in every form, as was noticeable before Cape Colony was reached. The building trade in Capetown itself has for years, I am told, been largely in the hands of Malays, who take contracts, and even employ white masons. The result is that coloured men here work as artificers, and earn 11s. or 12s. a day as masons, plasterers, &c. Cab-driving is also much in the hands of Malays. Generally the coloured population is prosperous.

An English lady, the wife of an high official, who had long been resident in the colony, took a more hopeful view of matters than I had lately heard. Her own family had prospered, and this may have affected her views, which are distinctly sanguine, as to the future prosperity of the colony, and so far a relief from the despondent tone that I have found to prevail. She says that the newspapers do their best to keep the sores open, but admits that the Progressive are no better thar the Bond newspapers in this respect. There are ways in which offence is unintentionally given. For instance, I am told that the Boers in the neighbourhood of Capetown are greatly annoyed because rifle-range practice goes on on Sundays—I suppose by the volunteers. The colonist, as a rule, has little regard for Sundays, whilst to the Boer the Sunday is as the old Scotch *Sawbath*. Our rule in permitting such a thing is not appreciated by the Boers, whose regulations, if they had the power to make them on the subject, would probably be objected to by the British. The two points of view are as different as the British infatuation for and the Boers' abhorrence of shopkeeping and town life, and it is not easy to see how a Government imbued with either set of ideas will suit the other

The Civil Service does not seem to be well paid at the Cape, whilst rent is so high that it commonly absorbs 20 per cent. of an official's salary. Very large houses are not, however, proportionately expensive, owing to the limited demand for them. Just now a scheme is under consideration for raising civil servants' salaries, and facilitating their purchasing their houses. The opposition—with some truth, no doubt—say that the measure has been brought forward in view of the coming elections. Anyway, I have seen it stated since these notes were made that some measure of relief has been given to the Civil Service. Attempts to defraud the Customs are said to be not uncommon, and lately a large firm was, I was told, mulcted in £3,000 for an offence of the kind.

I drove from Wynberg to the Government garden and vineyard at Constantia. The drive was a pretty one, on a fairly good road, largely under pine and oak avenues, and amongst gardens and vineyards interspersed with pine, oak, and apparently plane forests, this being the show part of perhaps the most cultivated place in these colonies. The views of the spurs and wooded kloofs of Table Mountain, at the foot of which Constantia stands, are certainly very fine, and the old Dutch house, reached by a fine oak avenue, formerly the property of the Dutch Governor, Mr. Cloete, is a stately old place and well maintained by the Colonial Government, who work the vineyard as a sort of model one. We saw the press-house, but the floor was all wet and the day advanced, and as no one seemed to have anything to show us, we took a stroll among the vines, all covered with enormous bunches of red and white grapes. But we had soon to return to the house, for heavy rain came on just as we reached the vineyard, and continued with short breaks only. The housekeeper, an old Dutchwoman, was very civil, and at her request we took a lady and child back with us on our covered cart. The lady, an Englishwoman, had then been in South Africa two months only, but had, three years before, been in the colony, the interval having been spent in Australia, which she greatly preferred to South Africa. She said that the influx of Australians was due to drought and bad times at the Antipodes.

On the next day I made inquiries on behalf of a friend who had an idea of coming to South Africa to farm. The gentleman I consulted had himself done well in that line, but he said that if he had to start again now he would not come here. Not only are grave political questions still unsolved, but untold diseases and difficulties confront the farmer. In fact, there is no farming as understood either in India or England. Nearly all the white man's food is imported; droughts, locusts, cattle diseases, ticks, flies, and other worries dog the flockmaster's feet at every step. It is only by discarding all European methods that success is obtainable.

There does not seem to be any kind of doubt that Mr. Chamberlain's visit has done much good. One of the permanent officials, who has as many Dutch as English friends, says that he believes that but for it civil war would have broken out, especially if any attempt had been made to set aside the colony's constitution. He added that with so long a line of coast the import of arms could not have been stopped. If the extreme men who keep the newspapers going would only quiet down, he thinks that permanent peace might follow, there being many Moderates on both sides. He, though a Britisher, considers the Dutch to be the most permanent and respectable element in South Africa. The opinion of non-officials of standing is that whilst the Dutch would not altogether prevail, the British, if they wished to prosper, would be compelled to make friends with the Dutch, and treat them as equals, which is just what they intensely object to doing. On the other hand, the Dutch are determined to have equal opportunities in every way with the British. In very many callings a knowledge of Dutch is of great advantage, not only in dealing with the Dutch, but also as regards the Kaffirs and coloured men, who can generally talk Dutch, and frequently no other language. Much Dutch business can only be done through Dutch mercantile firms.

In Capetown every one, irrespective of colour, can get a trading licence, so that the coloured races have a fair chance, with the result that the Malays almost monopolise the tailoring and plastering trades; and, as I have previously remarked, they do a good bit of cab-driving. They are clean and sober, and in many respects superior to the lower classes of Europeans. They all talk Dutch.

A Dutchman of influence told me that Mr. Chamberlain's visit had certainly done good, especially as it had opened his eyes to the real state of things in South Africa.

Mr. Hoffmeyer's circular would also do some good with certain people, but to forget the loss of wife, children, and property is not possible. He thinks that the stupefied and silent attitude of many of the Transvaal Boers is much more to be feared than the tall talk of the Cape politicians and newspaper writers of either side. He could not, when lately in the districts some way out from Pretoria, get a single Boer to talk about politics. They gave no sign that they had even heard of Kruger, Milner, or Chamberlain. They simply sat still and never spoke. He drove out forty miles to see an old Dutch friend, and found him living under a few corrugated iron sheets. He asked him why he had not commenced to rebuild his house. The reply was, "I shall never build another house. This shed will do for my lifetime, and I do not want another to be burnt over my head, so I intend now to live my life as you find me." This spirit, my friend says, is a bad sign, and no doubt it is.

The Colonial Secretary had long private interviews with Messrs. Hoffmeyer, Sauer, De Villiers, and others, and seems to have satisfied them that he was not going to let the British do "big dog" over the Dutch, as was avowedly Lord Milner's policy. This attitude of Mr. Chamberlain has no doubt influenced the Dutch for good. My friend, however, says that there is as much boycotting by the British as the Dutch, and that this can be seen in the clubs. Milner's young Balliol men are utterly inexperienced, and have got all the departments into a terrible mess; the railways are no better. The new Government, according to him, is likely to be enormously expensive, and people are wondering where the money will come from, or on what authority a few mine-owners offered the subvention of thirty millions. My friend adds that the new Government House at Pretoria is to be built on ground for which £40,000 has been paid, and that the building will cost as much, against £300 a year given as house rent to Kruger, whose salary was £7,000, against £11,000 paid to Lord Milner, not counting Sir A. Lawley. All the young boys from England get high salaries, so that the financial outlook is not regarded by the old hands as encouraging. The elections are likely to be exciting, and I am told that politics and drink will both run high. My friend concluded his remarks with the observation that South Africa is no place for married life, bachelors being far more comfortable. The opposition newspapers are not easy to obtain, but I gather that the Boers and British workmen are likely to be on one side and the Rand and De Beers capitalists on the other.

The municipal management of their affairs is said not to be more satisfactory than the Government management of the country. On the occasion of a recent large fire, out of thirty-two firemen only eight turned up, of whom two, including the engine-driver, were on arrival drunk and incapable. The superintendent's view of the matter was that he had sent all the men off and had no further concern in the business.

CHAPTER XI

Voyage home—A doctor on the concentration camps—Mr. Chamberlain's speeches to Progressives at Capetown not fully reported—An American on Kaffirs, colonials, and others—A colonial lady's views—The coming native war—Capabilities of Kaffirs—Slackness in business houses at Capetown—The Transvaal Railway Company—Indians indispensable in Natal—Boers more united and confident than they were before the war—Military officer's objection to South Africa—A colonial's view of the situation—Coloured races in Cape Colony—Nurse's experience—Madeira.

My journey to England started auspiciously, the ship steady and the weather warm and comfortable. One of the passengers, a genial Irishman, a city man, who had made the journey for the benefit of his health, told me that he now understood why so many youths who were out in the war had returned to England, and that on all sides he was informed that it was no use trying to disguise the fact that South Africa must eventually be dominated by persons of Dutch descent, who were not only numerically stronger but owned most of the land. Both at Pretoria and Johannesburg he thought that he had noticed a growing feeling that might unite the Boers and British workmen against the capitalists. A Cape official of high standing told me that the gold and diamond kings had bought up most of the newspapers, and were bent on being the real rulers of South Africa. The same combination which had never given Mr. Kruger's Government any peace still existed, and dominated not only the Cape newspapers, but most of the London ones also. At present they are lying low, but a campaign to introduce forced labour, which will in reality be slavery, will certainly be opened so soon as the coast is clear; newspaper articles preparing for it are already appearing.

The passengers are fortunately quiet people, and games are pursued in moderation without the aid of sweeps or other betting abominations. Amongst the passengers is a doctor who held a Government billet during the war, and was employed during the greater part of the time in a Boer camp, but was for four months at St. Helena. He is very angry at the stubbornness of the two hundred who still refuse to take the oath, whom he thinks should be treated with Russian severity. The men, he says, are nothing to the women, who are veritable viragos, and caused the war to be so long prolonged. But for the women the men would have given in long before they did so; their furious womankind would not, however, hear of it, and kept sending messages to fight on, fight ever. The doctor says he never saw such viragos. He does not think the two races will amalgamate for two generations at least, and clinched his opinion with an anecdote: A Belgian doctor, who has no children of his own, asked a Boer woman—in chaff, no doubt—to give him her baby and he would adopt it. She said, "No, you would not bring him up properly, as I shall." "How so?" he asked. "Why," she said, "the first words I shall teach him will be, 'shoot, shoot, shoot the English.'" "What are you to do with such people?" he said; and he sighed once more for a Czar who would do—well, I do not quite know what, nor does he.

I hear that Mr. Chamberlain's speeches to his Progressive friends were not fully reported, more especially his objections to Dr. Jim as their leader, and to the incorrectness of some of the statements they made.

An American, who has been employed in a Rand mine for a year, gave me his views at length. He laughs at the colonial notion that they can build up a nation by sitting down and watching Kaffirs work, and sees clearly through the cant about the labour difficulty and the need to force Kaffirs to work. He seems to like the Kaffirs, and, so far as mining is concerned, puts them ahead of all the labour he found in South Africa, where he says the English are not only wedded to the notion that good and bad workmen should get the same wages, but infect the natives, who naturally copy them, with the same ideas. The Kaffirs, if properly treated, are easily managed, and will do as they are told. Australians, he says, are much better workers than either English or South African colonials, and Boers are no good at all. The Australians, he says, have some of the American push in them. He explained the compound system, under which Kaffirs are employed in the Rand mines. If properly worked it seems to be fair enough. The "boys" live in these compounds but are free to move about as they like not being shut in, as is the case at the Kimberley diamond mines. There is a "compound keeper," who is usually a colonial who knows the natives and their language well, having formerly been a recruiting agent. He gets from £30 to £35 a month, and at times up to £40 on the very big mines. He keeps the "boys'" wages tickets and their accounts, and pays them, and this is done honestly. The "boys" are paid by shifts, and get the amount due at the end of every thirty shifts. They now get the original pay that was reduced after the war, and it runs from 1s. 3d. to 3s. a day, besides food and lodging. The food is ample and good, and cannot, in fact, be given in full when the "boys" arrive emaciated from their kraals, or they would over-eat themselves. There are certain head men amongst them known as mining chiefs, through whom, I understand, the compound keeper deals with the "boys." They are usually very fine, well-built men, the Zulus particularly, and these and the Basutos are the most intelligent, the Zulus making the best house servants. None of the South African natives like working underground, and there is much difficulty in getting the Zulus to go underground at all. The work is hard, and leads to lung sickness and many deaths, both amongst the "boys" and the white miners, who are all skilled workmen. Accidents are numerous, and the surgeons do not use anæsthetics, taking off arms and legs without them, which my informant looked on as rather brutal, though the Kaffirs do not expect anything else, and probably do not suffer from such treatment as Europeans would. My American friend thinks, as many do, that the mining magnates have not really desired to get labour, for manipulating purposes as he puts it, but he believes that they will eventually get Chinese labour, when the Kaffirs will disappear from the mines. He says that many of the latter are extremely fine men, and make good strikers in the smith's shops, where they like to try their hands on a bit of iron. I asked if they were not teachable, and he said, "Certainly, but that is just what the colonials dread and try to prevent." The "boys" save a good deal of money, which they lay out in clothes and in jewellery, buying in the small Jew shops that are found all round the compounds. They get clothes fairly cheaply, but are badly robbed in cheap useless watches and jewellery. I myself noticed a lot of watches being auctioned by sharpers in all the market places. Before the war the "boys" used to enter into engagements for from one to three years, but now they take on for six months only. The Kaffirs made money during the war, some of them now cashing cheques for £100, and even more. My American friend is inclined to think that the many-wife habit is not without some merits. Early marriage is not allowed, and morality is strict among the Zulus. There is no getting away from the fact that the Zulus are physically probably quite the finest race in the world, and there are other customs which make the practice less objectionable than at first sight appears to be the case.

The passage to Madeira was smooth and uneventful, and I spent my time in getting what information I could from my fellow-passengers. A colonial lady was very communicative, and did not give me a cheerful account of the Transvaal in peace or war. Her views, for which, however, I should be disinclined to make myself responsible, are—(1) That commercial morality is at the very lowest ebb. That any honest man must go to the wall. That the only idea of the Englishman in the Transvaal is to make money, as fast as possible, and to get away from the country. (2) That there is no question of Lord Milner's honest intentions, but that, as it is not possible for him to please any one of the different sets of dishonest, self-seeking men, he is unpopular all round. (3) That the Home Government has no consistent policy. Promises are constantly made and as frequently broken. (4) That there was, during the war, no end of loot and destruction, frequently without any cause. Houses were occupied by British officers without any rent being paid, whilst in some cases property was allowed to be made away with. The British taxpayer is now paying for this want of military discipline. (5) The British South African Constabulary is a very expensive and very inefficient force. The colonials will certainly object to keeping it on so soon as they have the power to do so. (6) That the privates, who get 5s. a day and rations, are rapidly marrying Boer girls and will eventually either run away and leave their wives behind them—which she thinks many will do—or become Boers themselves. (7) That Lord Milner's young men—the Kindergarten school—are extremely helpless, ignorant, and expensive. (8) That the reason why many Boers in exile have not taken the oath is because their wives will not allow them to do so. (9) That the Boers will certainly *trek* away from the Hebrew civilisation of Johannesburg to the outlying districts—the further away the better. (10) That the girl teachers brought out to teach the Boers occupy themselves in anything but their proper work, and that generally they are useless for the purpose for which they have been engaged. (11) That the payment of debts, except by the farming Boers, is irregular; that the same man frequently becomes bankrupt two or three times; and that it is next to impossible to run in a dishonest man, as the generality of people feel that it might be their own turn next, and are consequently inclined to sympathise with the "unfortunate." (12) That the real fault of Kruger's Government was in the Hollanders he brought over, most of whom have left, and are only returning very slowly. It is difficult to see how

Kruger could avoid employing Hollanders, as very few British colonials could speak Dutch, and the Boers themselves had not the necessary training or education. If some of the Hollanders were not immaculate, it is equally certain that the standard of honesty amongst them was quite up to the standard of the country. My own observations to the lady were that the war had happily done one thing, and that effectually: it had made it clear that the British must get on with the Dutch, who will eventually be the ruling race in South Africa. The lady took this view of the question herself, but when I said that I hoped it would prevent war in the future, she at once said, "Oh, but there will be a native war." That idea seems to be universal, and I trust that in that event the British will be on the side of justice, but I doubt this, because the natives have no one to speak for them, whilst the white men in South Africa are sparing of the truth when their interests are involved. Hence little reliable information is likely to reach the British public.

My American friend has been giving me further information about the Kaffirs, in regard to their intelligence and capability, respecting which I have received diverse views from various people—Dutch and English. Some said they were stupid and slow in picking up skilled forms of labour, whereas others had told me that they were quite intelligent; in fact, that of an equal number of country-bred town boys and Kaffirs, the latter probably had the best heads. My friend said the last view was his matured opinion, and he had studied them carefully. When he first came from America he did not think that the Kaffir was a satisfactory servant, and though his opinion has been much modified, he thought so still. But the cause of his inefficiency, so far as it is real, is that the Kaffir has not fair play. He has sufficient intelligence, but it is not good for him to know too much. In explanation he said that, if a white man saw a Kaffir using a file or making himself handy with tools, he would "knock him about," saying that was a white man's job, and not a Kaffir's. All the same, he added, "when out of sight, the white man will often let a Kaffir do a good deal of his work for him," and the way in which the latter often brings just the tools required showed that he must know a good deal. A white workman always has two or three Kaffirs in attendance on him, and just now the whites are living in some dread that new laws may open up a field for the improvement of the Kaffirs.

The slackness in Capetown, even in business houses and banks, is the subject of general comment. Even the ships' papers, I am told, come on board in such a mess that it takes two or three days to put them straight. The large liners apparently usually come home empty, since the South African colonist is not enterprising enough to start any manufactures, or even to grow his own food. These mail steamers carry forty to fifty tons of eggs every week to Capetown from the little island of Madeira, and South Africa is, to all intents and purposes, a huge desert.

A gentleman of Dutch descent on board, who has been many years in the Transvaal, about half in Pretoria, and latterly in Johannesburg, seemed to be freer than usual from prejudice, and greatly blamed the Hollander directors of the Transvaal Railway Company for supporting, and, as he seemed to think, really originating the Boer circular ordering their employés out on commando, instead of remaining as neutral railway hands. He is very much down on Lord Milner, not that he does not believe he is an upright and well-meaning administrator, but he says that the High Commissioner has a knack of getting round him the poorest and most useless of assistants, and that he puts himself so completely into the hands of the mining magnates that no one else can get a chance of having their opinions listened to. He is habitually advised by people who know nothing of the colony, and this results in his bringing out the most unworkable of ordinances, not a single one of which has not, immediately after issue, either to be cancelled or modified, for which he thinks Lord Milner's chief advisers are largely to blame. The Johannesburg Town Council is, he says, the laughing-stock of everybody, and even a scandal. He also told me that whereas Indians are accused of living in a dirty manner, yet the fault really lies with those who do not enforce cleanliness, and who do not, to begin with, clean the streets and drains in the parts of the town where the Indians live. The fact is that the part of Johannesburg where these wretched people live is wanted for railway purposes, and accordingly the cry of their insanitary habits has been raised. My friend said that he had himself known the town authorities to cart refuse to the Indian quarter and deposit it there. He sees clearly enough that the only possible way of making a country of South Africa is to open it unreservedly to all comers, Indians included, with no restrictions as to the trade or work they are allowed to take up. There would then soon be no difficulty in getting artisans or labour of any kind. He is strongly in favour of representative government being given quickly, but he does not, I think, see that representative government and fair play to the coloured people are under present circumstances impossible. If it is given, I trust that the Government of India will stop all emigration to South Africa, as they ought to do at once to Natal.

Natal, my Hollander friend truly says, cannot possibly get on without Indians, and the Government of India have it in their power to force Natal to treat Indians fairly, a fact which Lord Curzon ought to know and act on, for it is beyond doubt. My friend says that all that the Natal people did during the war was to enrich themselves to an enormous extent, whilst he does not believe that a single Natalian lost his life in action. His view is that it was a great mistake not making peace immediately Pretoria was reached, for the Boers then thought they were beaten, and wanted peace. Now, he says, they feel and believe that they are the most powerful element in South Africa, and that so much is this the case, that it will not even be necessary for them to fight again, because their superiority has already become apparent, whilst, according to their belief, it will become more and more evident to all as they increase in numbers.

The Boers have no feeling that they have been beaten, except by temporary exhaustion, and never before were the Dutch so united and confident in themselves as they are to-day. The other side feel that such is the case, and this is perhaps of more importance than what the Dutch think, as the colonials now know that if permanent peace is to result, they must make friends with the Dutch. My friend roundly accused the mining magnates—who had no interest in the country beyond what they could extract from it—of having overthrown the late Government for their own purposes, and of now being steadily engaged in plotting to get their own way or to overthrow the present Government. He was doubtful as to whether they would or would not succeed, as they have unquestionably enormous power, both in South Africa and London.

All the military officers on board seem strongly to object to soldiering in South Africa, on the ground of the expensiveness of the place, and partly on account of the unfriendly treatment they receive from the colonials. Soldiers frequently claim their discharge, and bring in offers of twelve to fifteen shillings a day against 11s. 6d., the pay of a subaltern. It is not wonderful, therefore, that officers find their positions trying, and fear the effect of such circumstances on discipline. The General has, it appears, recommended considerably increased emoluments, according to rank. The response has been an extra shilling a day all round. In a country so abnormal that a mason gets from 17s. to 27s. 6d. a day, and will not even then go to the suburbs unless a carriage is sent for him, it is plain that something more will have to be done.

I got the colonial view of matters from a Cape business man, who had risen in the world. He believes that the Dutch will have another try on yet, but said that of course England would see that they were "kept in their place." I ventured to doubt whether Great Britain would go on fighting for ever, whereupon he remarked that it would be a very uncomfortable matter for the Progressives if they did not receive British support. He had nothing to say against the Boers, except that they did not want progress, they only wanted to smoke on their own *stoops* and let Kaffirs bring in their corn. They did not want railways. He admitted that the Boers were, physically speaking, splendid men, and he was unable to account for their build and appearance if they led an idle, lazy life. The Bond, he thought, would certainly have a majority in the legislature after the next election.

I am told that in Cape Colony all colours and races are absolutely untrammelled in the matter of trade, the Malays taking the lead amongst the coloured people. One Malay has set up quite a fine shopfront in Capetown, and another has a large livery stable. They get the best education open to them at mission schools, Roman Catholic schools especially. The higher schools and colleges are not open to coloured persons, but as they, as well as most of the Indians or at any rate the better class of them, are Mohammedans who do not desire higher education, it does not matter, at any rate for the present, and they feel no grievance in being excluded. Many of them have votes, and they are now forming a political association, and will, in time, no doubt make their influence felt.

Some nurses returning home do not seem to have a high opinion of the manners and customs of the colonials, and on it being suggested to them that possibly their deficiencies in this respect might be derived from early contact with natives, one of them said that this was not at all likely, because her experience in the close relationship which life in hospitals renders obligatory convinced her that the native was by no means wanting in the virtues or decencies of life. She was quite unable to give any reasons, but had no doubt as to the fact.

Our stay of a few hours at Madeira was an agreeable interlude in the voyage. I was quite charmed with this beautiful island, rising in steep slopes almost directly out of the Atlantic to peaks that in spring at least are covered with patches of snow. The houses are built strictly after Portuguese patterns, and are embedded in gardens, where the most lovely flowers run riot in great abundance, love of gardening being everywhere apparent. Roses, arum lilies, geraniums, verbenas, and the dark red bougainvillæa, with innumerable others, were in splendid blossom, so were wistirias, trained over trellis roofs like vines, and giving out large areas of colour. The streets are cobbled with small pebbles, over which sledges are drawn, both by bullocks and men. A cogwheel railway goes up the mountain to a height of 2,000 ft. The alternative, which we adopted, is up a road having a slope of about one in eight, in a sleigh drawn by four bullocks. It is a slow process, but the route is pleasant, between terraced gardens. The journey back was by hand sleighs at a tremendous pace. The hills are all terraced and highly cultivated, sugarcane and potatoes being the favourite crops. The town below is clean and well kept, the shops good, and the people nice and civil. They have time for such old-world habits, and as I always notice in Portuguese places, there is a great air of quiet comfort and repose. They may not be a pushing, money-making race, but they appear to get a good deal more decent comfort and enjoyment out of their poverty than many more progressive races extract out of their wealth. It is extremely wonderful to find a place for all the world like an Indian hill station within four days of London. I can hardly imagine a nicer change than to move over and spend a month there in winter. There are some very nice and well-kept public gardens, where the flora looks just like that of the tropics.

A gentleman who came on board at Madeira, where he has spent five weeks, speaks very highly of the island. The climate he describes as always warm and comfortable. You can sit in the verandah all day and never need shut the windows. In the summer residents move up the mountains, which rise to a height of between 5,000 ft. and 6,000 ft. The hotels are comfortable, with good hot and cold water baths, and the usual charge is from 10s. to 12s. a day. Flowers, fruit, and vegetables are plentiful, but the meat is tough; the bread and butter good. Some African servants are employed. Houses (villas) can be got for about £50 a year, and some English people keep one and come out yearly. Portuguese servants are easily obtained. The island near the sea is never cold, and sugarcane crops follow each other all the year round. Sheep and cattle are fed up on the mountains. An alternative way of reaching Madeira is to go *viâ* Paris, Madrid, and Lisbon, whence daily packets do the journey in thirty or forty hours. Our journey from Madeira to Southampton was such as to lead me to think that it is desirable to make it as short as possible.

CHAPTER XII

Summary and Author's Conclusions.

THE foregoing narrative gives an account of my tour and the impressions it left on my mind. It was my object in making this inquiry to ascertain, as far as possible, the views most common amongst those living on the spot, and this could only be arrived at by hearing and noting the views of the people I came across from day to day. There is, therefore, I fear, much repetition, but this is unavoidable, as many of the persons with whom I conversed held the same opinion—perhaps differently expressed—as to the measures required for the development and pacification of South Africa. The conclusions drawn by me from the information I received and from my own observations have been frequently indicated, but it is perhaps well that I should finish these notes by summarising the points which seem to me to be most worthy of notice.

1. The first and foremost conclusion at which I arrived is that South Africa—hard as the sentence may sound to South Africans—is essentially, in common parlance, a "black country." In Natal, and in fact everywhere, the hard manual labour is done by coloured races, and whatever progress has been made is mainly due to them. Until Indians were introduced into Natal absolutely no progress was made with agriculture in that colony; in fact, as an Indian out there remarked to me—and all the white people to whom I quoted his remark confirmed his statement—cabbages even

were not grown until they showed the white people how to grow them. A white workman, even now, has generally one or two coloured assistants in attendance on him.

2. Another conclusion of, I think, supreme importance to the British taxpayer is that Cape Colony and Natal have grown extremely rich on the late war. Without periodic wars, Natal, with its present restrictions on immigration—continually being increased in stringency—will go backwards rather than forwards, as has been the case with it in the past during each period of peace. Another war, which is already in process of being written up, will, it it comes off, doubtless give the Colony a spurt again, just as the Zulu War did in 1878.

3. The expression, "Native War," has frequently appeared in these notes, and I may add that every one is talking of the same as an event which is likely to occur in the near future—most men say, certain to occur; but it is important to observe that the colonists—certainly those in Natal—have not the remotest intention of paying for it. On the contrary, they mean Great Britain to "pay the piper," although they are to "call the tune," and at the same time to again reap such profits as war has invariably brought them in the past.

4. On the other hand, looked at from a non-colonial point of view, there is no reason for a native war, if the coloured races are treated with any semblance of justice. In fact, there would be no dissatisfaction amongst the native races if the coloured people were allowed such privileges as, until the recent immigration law, they had long enjoyed in Cape Colony. These races do not ask to be put on a social or political equality with the whites, but they do ask that they may be governed with fairness and justice, and that they may have a chance of reaping the fruits of their own industry, frugality, and enterprise. They are not at all keen on taking any share in the government themselves; in fact, all their traditions are in favour of good government by people of a stronger political fibre than characterises themselves rather than of self-government, but they are

beginning to realise that there is no chance of their receiving fair treatment unless a certain proportion of them have votes, and to this extent at least participate in the government of the country. There is not the slightest doubt that they are right, for there is no other means that I can see by which they can hope to secure for themselves fair and equitable treatment.

5. That the present position of the coloured races in the lately annexed provinces is intolerable, and it is to be recollected that these provinces are directly under the government of Great Britain itself, so that this responsibility cannot be shirked, and must be faced. Neither Kaffirs nor Indians can hold land in these provinces; they are practically prohibited from exercising any skilled trades, whilst altogether inadequate means are taken to provide education for their children, notwithstanding that a special tax is placed on them, for which, it is frequently asserted, they get a return in good and civilised government. Again, so far as Indians now arriving in South Africa are concerned, they are not permitted to settle in a country which their labour is enriching, and, in the case of Natal, it may be said, has created.

6. That it is a scandal that British subjects should be put in a position of inferiority to foreigners in no way their superiors in either intellectual or moral qualifications, or even in point of education, as now happens under the existing laws.

7. That it is the duty of the Indian Government to protect their own subjects, and they have the power to do so, as they can prohibit emigration unless the Indians receive fair treatment. Such fair treatment must include the right to hold land and to practise any trade after their indentures have expired. If the Indian Government take action in this direction they are bound to succeed, because Natal, at any rate, as every colonist admits, cannot possibly thrive without Indian help.

8. That in granting self-government to the new colonies, every effort should be made to secure proper treatment for

all British subjects whatever their colour, with which object an agreement should be entered into that no measures penalizing the coloured races should be introduced for at least seven years after the grant of self-government. This limited term is proposed because it is realised that, after once self-government has been granted, the colonies must in the long run work out their own salvation.

9. That of the white races now in South Africa, the Boers are physically, mentally, and morally the best suited to successfully colonise that country. They share, however, to a considerable extent with the other white races, a general repugnance to hard physical labour, this not improbably being a legacy from the days of slavery in which they were nursed. They are, moreover, the only white race in South Africa willing to live in the wilds—the illimitable veldt that exercises such a transcendental effect on Mr. Joseph Chamberlain—and they have an invincible repugnance to town careers. This characteristic promises to greatly increase their permanent influence in the country.

10. That one effect of the war has been to unite the various branches of the Dutch element in South Africa to an extent never before attained. It is notorious that previous to the war little love was lost between the Cape Dutch and the Transvaal burghers, who were at times on the verge of open hostilities, but that day has now gone.

11. That the only possible safe system of administering self-governing colonies is to let the majority rule, and, much as they may dislike it, the colonists of British descent will have to recognise their fellow-subjects of Dutch origin as fully their equals in every respect. It may be added that where English colonists marry Dutch women—and such unions have been common in the past, whilst even now they are not rare—it is remarkable that the children inherit the proclivities of their mothers, and frequently become far more Dutch than the Dutch themselves.

12. It is possible that, if the Dutch are treated as equals and given equal rights, that the country will settle down in

time as a self-governing colony, just as Lower Canada has done; but even this is, in my opinion, not altogether certain, and, in any case, there will be no effusive loyalty. There is none, in fact, in Lower Canada, as those that know the country will, I doubt not, acknowledge. The loyalty of even the British colonists in South Africa is mainly a keen appreciation of benefits received, combined with a fervent hope for more in the future, at the cost of the British taxpayer.

13. That Mr. Chamberlain's visit was productive of good, chiefly owing to his decision not to suspend the Cape Colony Constitution, a step which would, had it been carried out, in all probability have brought on a civil war; but his visit was also beneficial in that he acquired a knowledge, to a far greater extent than before, of the real cause of unrest in South Africa. This unrest undoubtedly arose from the jealousy existing between the two white races, the British colonists being determined to domineer over the Dutch so long as they were sure of support from home, whilst the Dutch, on the other hand, were becoming more and more restive as they gradually felt their power and resented the assumption of superiority over them.

14. Into the actual causes of the late war it is not desirable to enter here further than to express the opinion that it ought never to have occurred, and that it was mainly engineered by capitalists for their own purposes, which I devoutly trust they will never attain. Further, I believe it would not have occurred if Mr. Chamberlain had made his visit to South Africa two years earlier than he did. I may add that I am fully aware that the Boers are as little inclined to treat coloured people fairly as the British colonists, and that I recognise that in self-governing colonies it is hopeless for the Mother Country to permanently insist on any regulations on the subject. But I think that, on the whole, the coloured races have a better chance with the Boers than with the other white colonists, because the Indians, at least, are in no sense competitors of the former, whilst, on the contrary, as

artisans and shopkeepers, they supply a want of the Boer farmers in furnishing them and their Kaffir farm servants with stores on far cheaper terms than could be got from dealers of other races. On the other hand, the Indians come into sharp competition with the shop-keeping classes, who, it is important to recollect, are now being almost entirely recruited from the south-east of Europe, who have been for a long time, and are still, swarming into South Africa. The extent to which this is happening is imperfectly known in England, where it is not recognised so much as it should be, that what are known as Uitlanders are for the most part non-British. Probably, for some time past, two-thirds of the people entering the new colonies are not emigrants from Great Britain or Ireland. With these people the Indians come into sharp and effective competition.

15. As a corollary to the statement made in No. 1, that South Africa should be considered as a "black country," I may observe that the British-born colonist has, as a rule, no intention of settling there. Like his representative in India, he hopes to return to England to end his days. His children who remain in the country are seldom equal to their parents in energy, ability, or character; the second generation, again, is far more degenerate; and there is just the same tendency for the race to die out in the third and fourth generations as is observable in India. The Boers have enormous families, and must, in the long run, preponderate in numbers in South Africa. The only deterioration noticeable in them is a disinclination for hard manual labour, which, as previously noted, is probably a relic of the slave-holding days, fostered by the feeling, always prevalent where coloured men are employed, that such labour is proper for blacks only. But although they rarely submit themselves to hard manual work, they lead rough and active out-of-door lives, as their stamina and appearances abundantly indicate, and their conduct in the defence of their country has indeed testified to the whole world.

Finally, if the attempt to keep South Africa a "white man's country" is persevered in, that part of the empire will never afford a very large market for British goods, as it will never be either thickly populated, or will, apart from its gold, its diamonds, and its wars, advance even in wealth. But for these it would long ago have been a *quantité negligible* in the British dominions, and it has, in point of fact, even with them, not built up a single industry, not excepting agriculture, which so far does not nearly afford food for its own sparse population. Cape Colony, but for the discovery of diamonds, was on the point of collapse years ago. That discovery alone saved it. Natal has been kept going by successive wars, and by the toll it levies on the stores forwarded through Durban to the Transvaal mines. Both the diamonds and the gold may last for many years yet, whilst the colonists will assuredly produce periodic wars if the Old Country will continue to pay for them, but, unless cheap coloured labour is really encouraged to work and increase in South Africa, by having the fruits of patience and industry freely and honourably secured to it, as is the case in India, it is futile to expect that any large permanent and increasing markets will be found, or that anything approaching the trade of India will ever be opened out in these Colonies. It is also not sufficiently understood at home that the gold-bearing mines in the Transvaal yield only very poor grade ore, and that this cannot possibly be worked to a profit on the enormously inflated stock to which the industry has been watered by promoters and gamblers, unless something approaching slave or forced labour is made use of. That is the real difficulty of the "labour question," so often lightly spoken of, and it is a very real difficulty indeed. The mining magnates know this well enough, and they also know that the investing public at home has of late years largely forsaken foreign stocks for South African gold investments. I hope, therefore, that the fear of heavy losses may not so blind the eyes of Great Britain as to cause it to permit the mining rulers to set up a system of forced labour grossly underpaid, for that alone is what the inveigling of Chinese or Indians into fenced compounds, on five years' indentures, on terms that will be wholly misunderstood by the victims before they reach South Africa, really amounts to. Such a system will be slavery hidden under a thin veil of hypocrisy, and will probably lead to bloodshed if it is permitted. It is to be hoped it never will be.